SQUADRONS!

No. 28

THE CONSOLIDATED B-24

LIBERATOR

- THE AUSTRALIANS -

PHIL H. LISTEMANN

ISBN: 979-1096490-30-1

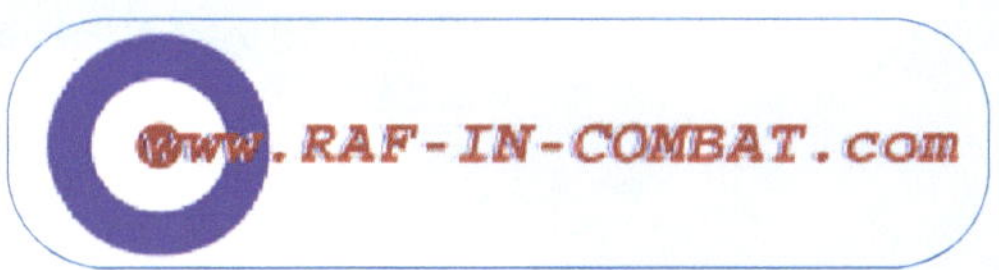

Colour profiles: Gaetan Marie/Bravo Bravo Aviation

Contributors & Acknowledgments:
Aviation Heritage Museum of Western Australia

GLOSSARY OF TERMS

PERSONEL :
(AUS)/RAF: Australian serving in the RAF
(BEL)/RAF: Belgian serving in the RAF
(CAN)/RAF: Canadian serving in the RAF
(CZ)/RAF: Czechoslovak serving in the RAF
(NFL)/RAF: Newfoundlander serving in the RAF
(NL)/RAF: Dutch serving in the RAF
(NZ)/RAF: New Zealander serving in the RAF
(POL)/RAF: Pole serving in the RAF
(RHO)/RAF: Rhodesian serving in the RAF
(SA)/RAF: South African serving in the RAF
(US)/RAF - RCAF : American serving in the RAF or RCAF

RANKS
G/C : Group Captain
W/C : Wing Commander
S/L : Squadron Leader
F/L : Flight Lieutenant
F/O : Flying Officer
P/O : Pilot Officer
W/O : Warrant Officer
F/Sgt : Flight Sergeant
Sgt : Sergeant
Cpl : Corporal
LAC : Leading Aircraftman

OTHER
ATA: Air Transport Auxiliary
CO : Commander
DFC : Distinguished Flying Cross
DFM : Distinguished Flying Medal
DSO : Distinguished Service Order
Eva. : Evaded
ORB : Operational Record Book
OTU : Operational Training Unit
PoW : Prisoner of War
PAF: Polish Air Force
RAF : Royal Air Force
RAAF : Royal Australian Air Force
RCAF : Royal Canadian Air Force
RNZAF : Royal New Zealand Air Force
SAAF : South African Air Force
s/d: Shot down
Sqn : Squadron
† : Killed

THE CONSOLIDATED B-24

The Consolidated B-24 Liberator was the most produced heavy bomber of WW2 with close to 19,000 units built. It made its first flight on 29 December 1939 and, in many aspects, such as its tricycle landing gear, was far more modern than the Boeing B-17 Flying Fortress. Initially, Consolidated was asked to consider production of the B-17, but its response was that a better aircraft could be designed and produced. The USAAC awarded a contract for a prototype on 30 March 1939, followed by a pre-production order, for evaluation, for seven YB-24s in April. Before the prototype had flown, another order was placed for 38 production aircraft (B-24A, C and D), Boeing receiving a similar order the same day. In 1940, the Anglo-French Purchasing Commission was allowed to examine the design. As a result, a letter-of-intent followed to purchase 165 B-24s with the denomination of LB-30.

The design was progressively improved during the war and Consolidated developed variants up to the XB-24N. The main and most produced variant was the B-24J. The B-24 proved to be versatile during the war, its major quality being its excellent operational range. It was an attractive candidate for long-range maritime patrols and the USN eventually took charge of close to 1000 B-24s under the denomination of PB4Y. The RAF also used the B-24 for General Reconnaissance (GR) duties and by the end of war it had become the RAF's main type used by land based GR squadrons in the UK and overseas. The RAF flew about 2,300 B-24s over nine marks (Liberator Mk.I to Mk.IX) during the war. They were used as bombers in the Middle East, southern Europe and Far East, in the maritime reconnaissance role, as electronic warfare platforms, and as transports. The RCAF was also a major user, mainly using aircraft coming from RAF batches, and the SAAF operated the Liberator under RAF command. Australia was another large user during the war, but without any connection to the UK orders. As far as the RAAF is concerned, the variants entered into the inventory were:

B-24D:

The first variant produced on a large scale and the first USAAC combat ready model. It was ordered from 1940 to 1942 and about 2,700 aircraft were built. With the RAF, the B-24D took up the denomination of Liberator Mk.III or Mk.V. They didn't have nose turrets when built, but later in the war many were modified in the field with a turret similar to later production models. That's what the Australians received from the Americans.

B-24J:

The B-24J was very similar to the B-24H which had introduced the nose turret on the production line. However, shortages of the Emerson nose turret of the B-24H required use of a modified, hydraulically-powered Consolidated A-6 turret in most J-model aircraft built at the San Diego and Fort Worth factories. The B-24J featured an improved autopilot (type C-1) and a bombsight of the M-1 series. The J-model was the only version built by all five factories involved in B-24 production. An impressive 6678 were built. The B-24H and B-24J became the Mk.VI in the RAF, but this denomination was never adopted by the RAAF.

B-24M A72-198 seen shortly after its arrival in Australia to be taken on charge. It was, numerically, the last B-24M in the RAAF's inventory, but not the last of that model to be accepted. It was taken on charge on 23 January 1945 and withdrawn from use in March 1946 to be eventually scrapped in December 1952. Its main assignment was to 1 Aircraft Performance Unit. *(AHM & WA)*

The crew of W/C 'Arch' Dunne (OC 23 Sqn) posing in front of a B-24L. Note the lightweight tail turret. Left to right: F/L Fred Barry Brown, F/L A.B. 'Buck' Buchanan (nose), F/L A.M. 'Monty' Yeomans (2nd pilot), W/C R.A. Dunne DFC (captain), S/L Sid Linehan (bomb aimer), F/O John Jamison (navigator), F/O R.E. Hensel (W/Op).
Front row: F/Sgt Griffin (tail), F/Sgt Bruce Smith (engineer), Sgt Perc Clegg (waist), and F/Sgt Tom Moore (belly).

B-24L:

Because of the excessively high gross weight of the B-24J, the USAAF pushed for a lighter version and the B-24L was the result. The Sperry ball turret was replaced by a floor ring mount with two .50 calibre (12.7 mm) machine guns, and the A-6B tail turret by an M-6A. Later aircraft were delivered from the factory without tail armament (to be installed locally) as needs differed from one theatre of operations to another. An A-6B, M-6A, or a manually-operated twin .50 calibre (12.7 mm) mounting (for less defended areas like in the Pacific) was installed at a depot before arrival at operational units. The L-model was only built at Willow Run and Consolidated's San Diego factory for a total of 1667 aircraft. Known as the Liberator Mk.VIII in RAF use, the RAAF never used this denomination.

B-24M:

This variant was an enhancement of the B-24L with further weight-saving measures. The B-24M used a more lightweight version of the A-6B tail turret, the A-6C. The waist gunner positions were left open and the retractable Sperry ventral ball turret was reintroduced. For better visibility from the flight deck, the windshield in Ford-built aircraft was replaced by a version with less framing from Block 20 onward. The B-24M became the last production model of the B-24. A number of the 2593 built flew from the factory to the scrapper. The RAAF was the only non-US recipient as the RAF did not receive the B-24M.

THE AUSTRALIAN LIBERATORS

The B-24 Liberator was active in the South West Pacific with the USAAF shortly after the Americans entered the war. American heavy bomb groups were based in Australia and the long-range of the B-24 was really appreciated. The Liberator was even found more suitable than the B-17 Flying Fortress which was eventually removed from combat in the area in 1943. The same year, production planning of the B-24 was such that the type was made available in large numbers to Commonwealth nations. To support the USAAF and to operate over New Guinea and the East Indies, it was agreed at the end of 1943 that the RAAF would form seven squadrons equipped with the Liberator.

The original intention was that the first RAAF B-24 unit formed would be No. 99 Squadron in March 1944. However, when the USAAF asked the RAAF to withdraw the Vultee Vengeance from frontline ops in the South West Pacific area, after only six weeks on operations, as the Vengeance was deemed unsuitable by the Americans, the RAAF had other ideas. Therefore, Nos. 21, 23 and 24 Squadrons, previously flying the Vengeance, were earmarked to be the first to be converted to the Liberator. They would be incorporated into a new command structure, No. 82 Wing. Later, in 1945, another new wing was formed, No. 85, with three squadrons – Nos. 12, 99 and 102. The other two units were No. 25 Squadron, used separately in a mostly anti-shipping role, and No. 102 Squadron which was still working up when the war in the Pacific ended. Alongside those seven squadrons, two Special Duties Flights, Nos. 200 and 201, were also formed. This was all possible because the RAAF was provided with no less than 287 B-24 Liberators. All received serials beginning with A72 as per the RAAF series. They were delivered between February 1944 and August 1945 and, if we ignore the first thirteen (**A72-1 to A72-13**), all were brand new. The first twelve were older B-24Ds handed over by the USAAF in Australia, all having been modified with a nose turret. These B-24Ds were war weary and suitable only for training. For example, A72-1 had more than 800 hours on the airframe when taken on RAAF charge in February 1944. For the remaining aircraft, the B-24J was to become the major type with 145 examples taken on charge (**A72-13, A72-31 to A72-68 and A72-300 to A72-405**), followed by the B-24L with 83 aircraft (**A72-69 to A72-142 and A72-149 to A72-157**) and 47 B-24Ms (**A72-143 to A72-148 and A72-158 to A72-198**). When the war ended in September 1945, the RAAF Liberators had performed over 1750 bombing, anti-shipping and special duty sorties, but the type was soon withdrawn from service as Australia did not have plans to use aircraft provided under the Lend Lease Act, nor pay for them. The Australian heavy bomber force would eventually be equipped with an Australian-built version of the Avro Lincoln.

TRAINING ON THE LIBERATOR

The first challenge the RAAF had to face was to train crews. Many Australians were already flying heavy bombers with the RAF in the UK, but nothing could be expected from a Bomber Command heavily engaged in the large-scale air offensive over Europe. Therefore, the only help, for training and combat experience to expedite the conversion of 24 Squadron, could come from the Americans and the Fifth Air Force based in Australia. A second course of five crews and a third of eight followed before the RAAF received its own B-24s for training purposes. When the first five RAAF Liberator crews completed their training at the end of January 1944, they were assigned to the USAAF's 43rd BG at Nadzab, in New Guinea, for combat training before transferring to the 380th BG for combat experience. This unit would take on the responsibility of building up a full strength RAAF B-24 squadron. The 380th BG was not the only American B-24 bomb group to contribute, but that unit was located in the combat area later covered by the Australian heavy bomber force. Eventually, 52 Australian crews served with the 380th BG (thirteen each in four successive 'courses') to acquire the necessary 100 combat hours over the full gamut of 380th missions. Most of the time they flew as full Australian aircrews, but it was common to see them flying as part of American crews as well. By January 1945, the last RAAF crews had completed their training with the 380th. Over the next two months the two Australian B-24 units took over the assignments of the 380th BG and transferred to Darwin prior to the Americans rejoining the Fifth Air Force for the move to the Philippines. Fourteen RAAF members were posted killed or missing in action while serving with the 380th BG. This figure includes one full crew.

In the meantime, the RAAF formed a dedicated unit on 15 February 1944 when No. 7 OTU was raised at Tocumwal, New South Wales. Command was temporarily given to S/L A. Hubbard who had served in the Middle East with Nos. 70 and 38 Squadrons before completing his tour with No. 460 (RAAF) Squadron of Bomber Command in the UK. The first two former USAAF B-24Ds (A72-7 and 8) arrived on the 21st and were joined in March by A72-3, 4, 5 and 9, and in April by A72-2 and 6. The last secondhand Liberators arrived in May (A72-1, 10 and 11) and A72-13, a B-24J, in July. Of these, three (A72-3, 6 and 7) were allocated as ground instruction airframes upon arrival and did not fly again. In July, the Liberator fleet was reinforced with new aircraft (A72-33, 45, 46). During the autumn, more B-24s were added to the inventory. The first Liberator training course finished on 2 June and the second commenced on the 11th. The third was designed to carry out the purpose of converting and selecting instructor pilots, all of whom were already qualified instructors, to be responsible for future pilot training at the OTU. The programme progressed well and by October the OTU was able to train 27 crews per month. Each course was of eight weeks duration and each crew received 120 hours of flying training. Upon completion of training at Tocumwal, crews proceeded to the Far East Air Force Combat Replacement and Training Center (CRTC) at Nadzab for a further forty or so hours of operational flying training, combat experience and 'tropicalisation' with the USAAF. Inevitably, the training process was far from a walk in the park, and accidents were frequent, but only one fatal crash was recorded while A72-128 was not repaired after a minor landing accident and only three other incidents led to an aircraft being written off. It was a rather huge unit

Supplied by the 5th AF in May 1944, B-24D 42-40522 became A72-6 with the RAAF, but never trained RAAF crews as it served as a ground instructional airframe with the Engine School at Point Cook. *(AHM & WA)*

as, in June 1945, 7 OTU had 1660 personnel and 54 Liberators on strength (and eleven Vengeances, an Oxford and five Kittyhawks). After VE-Day, orders were received that fifteen Liberators were to be converted to transports to assist with the return of prisoners of war to Australia. The unit was eventually disbanded on 30 November 1945. In all, fourteen operational training courses went through Tocumwal.

The aftermath of the crash of A72-123 on 19 January 1945. No major injuries were sustained by the crew. Despite intensive training, 7 OTU had a relatively low ratio of accidents during its existence compared to similar units.

Summary of the aircraft lost by accident - 7 OTU (RAAF)

Date	Pilot	S/N	Origin	Serial	Code	Fate
02.10.44	*Destroyed by fire on the ground*	-	-	**A72-1**	1	-
02.10.44	*Destroyed by fire on the ground*	-	-	**A72-4**	4	-
11.01.45	F/L Frank W. **Bottomer**	Aus. 405146	RAAF	**A72-8**	8	-
	F/O Francis J. **Sheehan**	Aus. 415688	RAAF			-
	P/O Robert G. **Roberston**	Aus. 2406	RAAF			-
	LAC Thomas J. **Shand**	Aus. 53435	RAAF			-
19.01.45	F/O John **Major**	Aus. 421496	RAAF	**A72-123**	123	-
	Five of rest of the crew of 12 slightly injured					
14.02.45	F/O Glen M. **Brugman**	Aus. 414758	RAAF	**A72-112**	112	-
	W/O Allen L. **Jones**	Aus. 14233	RAAF			†
	Sgt Raymond D. **Johnston***	Aus. 445230	RAAF			†
	Cpl George S.R. **McLeod**	Aus. 15381	RAAF			-
	Sgt William G. **Hobbs**	Aus. 441074	RAAF			-
	W/O Norman D. **Henderson**	Aus. 408819	RAAF			**Inj.**
	Sgt Leslie H. **Brown**	Aus. 431694	RAAF			-
	W/O Douglas L. **Simpson**	Aus. 402756	RAAF			-
	Sgt John A. **Wilson**	Aus. 431693	RAAF			-
	W/O Keith **Herman**	Aus. 415655	RAAF			-
	Sgt Donald K. **Mackenzie**	Aus. 444953	RAAF			-
16.04.45	F/L Eric J. **Merryweather**	Aus. 406659	RAAF	**A72-36**	36	-
	Rest of the crew not reported but safe					-
18.09.45	*No details available, but no casualties*			**A72-128**	128	-
	-					

*Died the next day

Total: 7

Two B-24s of 7 OTU during a training flight. Above is B-24L A72-89 and below is B-24L A72-92. Both were issued to 7 OTU at the end of October 1944 and both were transferred to 25 Sqn in January 1945. While A72-89 survived the war, A72-92 was lost on 28 July 1945 in the Celebes while serving with 21 Sqn.

Number of sorties: *ca.* 750

First operational sortie:
06.07.44
Last operational sortie:
12.08.45

Number of claims: 1.00

Total aircraft written-off: 10

Aircraft lost on operations: 9
Aircraft lost in accidents: 1

Squadron code letters:
GR

COMMANDING OFFICERS

S/L Richard L. Lewis	Aus. 406166	RAAF	...	17.06.44
W/C John B. Hampshire	Aus. 392	RAAF	17.06.44	06.03.45
W/C Russel E. Bell	Aus. 268	RAAF	06.03.45	...

SQUADRON USAGE

Number 24 Squadron was initially formed as a general-purpose squadron in June 1940 and, by the end of that year, was operating Lockheed Hudsons. It fought over Rabaul in 1942 and was wiped out. Reformed in Australia with various aircraft, it was maintained far from the frontline until it could be re-equipped with Vultee Vengeances. Flying them to Nadzab in New Guinea, the squadron supported Australian Kittyhawks for two months before returning to Lowood, Queensland, in March 1944 to become the first former Vengeance squadron to convert to the B-24 Liberator. For this, a new CO was appointed, W/C J.B. Hampshire, who replaced S/L R. Lewis. The first five B-24Js were allocated on 5 June and received a couple of days later (A72-31, A72-34, A72-35, A72-38 and A72-43). Before the end of the month, crews began to be posted in while more B-24s were taken on charge with the arrival of A72-39, A72-40, A72-41, A72-42. The squadron completed its move to Manbulloo, Northern Territory, by 27 June with nine B-24Js, three under the normal establishment. In July, the squadron, suffering from a lack of ground equipment, restricted its daily activity even though, as far as the B-24 was concerned, the squadron had finally reached its operational strength of twelve aircraft. In July, several Liberators were detached to Fenton where a few operational sorties were carried out. On 6 July, F/L C.E.R. Parsons and his crew took off in A72-39/GR-J for a special supply drop over western New

Two of 82 Wing's high ranking officers at Fenton in June 1945. Left, G/C D.W. Kingwell, officer commanding, and one of his squadron commanders, W/C R.E. Bell, 24 Sqn. Group Captain Kingwell was made a Companion of the DSO in June 1946 for his leadership of the wing, while W/C Bell earned the DFC in February 1946 for his actions with the squadron.

B-24J A72-34/GR-D, in flight during the summer of 1944, was among the first to be taken on charge by 24 Sqn. Sent away for overhaul in the middle of the autumn, it was then issued to 7 OTU before entering storage from January 1945. *(AHM & WA)*

Guinea. This first sortie was not successful because communications with the ground could not be established and the aircraft returned to base after a flight lasting 10 hours and 40 minutes. The same aircraft and crew returned on the 13th for a successful drop. On 27 July, the squadron was ordered to proceed to Darwin with seven Liberators to participate in a joint mission with the 380th BG. However, when they arrived, and before the briefing took place, all of the B-24s were declared unserviceable for operations, due to mechanical defects, by the technical officer of the 531st BS. All of the aircraft returned to base the following morning. Two shipping searches were carried out on 3 August, with both aircraft following different flightpaths (A72-31/GR-A and A72-37), and another the following day (A72-41). Liberator A72-37, with F/L T.S. Erikson and crew - T.S Erikson was Norwegian-born Australian -, was the first of its type in RAAF service to drop bombs on a target when a 300 ton schooner was attacked from 5000 feet and a nearby village also bombed. On the 4th, it was the turn of F/O M.D. Frecker to attack a target when he made two bombing runs (strafing at the same time) on a 1500 ton merchant vessel and followed up with another two strafing runs. None of the bombs hit the vessel and 1000 rounds were fired at it. Moderate light anti-aircraft fire was encountered and proved accurate as F/O B.J. Middleton, the rear gunner, was killed instantly by an explosive shell that entered the door of the rear turret. It is believed that he was killed on the third pass as his guns remained silent after that. Middleton, who had been awarded the DFM in 1943 while serving with No. 49 Squadron in Bomber Command, became the first member of the squadron to be killed on active service since it re-equipped with B-24s. Until the end of August, close to forty similar sorties were flown, but few sightings made, and less attacks performed. During one on the 17th, with F/L A.J. Rayment and crew in A72-32/GR-B, the aircraft was slightly damaged by return fire. On the 19th, F/O M.D. Frecker and crew in A72-35 flew an uneventful sortie, but, on the 24th, and in the same aircraft flown by Frecker, F/O H.D. Carrigan and crew attacked a possible submarine. Bombs were dropped on a probable camp area later that day by F/L R.F. Overheu and his crew in A72-34/GR-D as they headed for home. This kind of action, dropping bombs on targets of opportunity on the return journey, became more or less the rule by the end of August. Aside from the search missions, the squadron was asked to carry out two special ops from Darwin on the 9th and 12th. Three B-24s were involved each time and both operations were successful.

On 1 September, the squadron moved to Fenton and sorties resumed on the 3rd. On 6 September, the first B-24 was lost when A72-39, flown by F/L C.E.R. Parsons, burst its left tyre on return from a shipping search. The pilot was unable to prevent the aircraft from careering into a large ditch. The landing gear collapsed, causing considerable damage, and the aircraft was written-off and stripped for spares. None on board were injured. The operational routine continued, but, on the 9th, the first bombing strike was flown, S/L L.W. Manning, the A Flight CO, leading two boxes of three B-24s. This strike was flown in conjunction with the 380th BG, an arrangement that would be repeated in the future. The target was the Laha aerodrome and the bombers were to try to neutralise the strip and the aircraft based there. The op was carried out without incident. Another strike was flown on the 16th, the target this time being Khadari aerodrome. This raid was led by the other flight commander, S/L M.C. Combe, and was followed by a third with six B-24s attacking Hareokoe aerodrome. Between the raids, the squadron maintained its shipping search duties.

October started with another raid of six B-24s, led by W/C Hampshire, to destroy the airstrip at Laha and the aircraft grounded there. Another raid was carried out on the night of the 2nd, the target being ground installations at Macassar. The squadron participated in five more raids using six Liberators (8th, 10th, 20th, 24th and 31st) in addition to its usual shipping searches. Close to sixty sorties were flown in October. During the month, the squadron was notified that the B-24Js they were flying would be replaced by new B-24Ls. The first was collected on 2 November by the CO. This change progressed as aircraft became available and by the end of the month the squadron was flying both types even though the L-model made up the bulk of the squadron's inventory. Actually, the J-model never disappeared completely with a few remaining on strength until the type was retired. As not all of the B-24Js were sent back when new aircraft arrived, the squadron had an excess of machines for a couple of months. On the 13th, the squadron was officially put under the administrative control of 82 Wing. From the operational side, November and December continued as October did with more than 100 sorties achieved before the end of the year. The squadron had now entered an established routine when New Year 1945 was celebrated. That was sadly disrupted on 23 January when A72-70, sent on a shipping search, failed to return. Pilot Officer K.H. Richards and his crew were posted missing. Ten days later, on 2 February, another dramatic accident occurred. Liberator A72-88, captained by F/L A.A. Cambridge, was returning from an attack on Japanese shipping. It arrived over Fenton in hazy weather conditions and visibility down to about one mile. On the downwind leg of the circuit, Cambridge was unable to see the flarepath. On turning into the wind, the flarepath was not visible above 700 feet. The aircraft was far to the left of the strip. The Liberator acknowledged the message warning of this and indicated that another circuit would be made. It overshot and retracted the undercarriage. At the same time the B-24 violently swung to the left because engines 1, 2 and 3 lost oil pressure while that of the starboard outer fluctuated. Cambridge tried to maintain height on the one engine capable of full power, but this simply was not enough. Two crewmen were killed in the ensuing crash, while the others were injured to varying degrees. The squadron returned to its routine and, on 25 February, while patrolling for reported enemy vessels at Salah Bay, the B-24 captained by F/L E.V. Ford was attacked by a Japanese fighter identified as an 'Oscar'. It was first seen by the left waist gunner, Sgt W.W. Cayer, flying parallel to the Liberator (A72-77). When it was sighted, the B-24 was carrying out its third strafing run on a Japanese motor truck that was eventually destroyed by fire. On pulling out from these attacks, and at an altitude of 1500 feet, the enemy fighter made a head-on attack, closing to 150 yards. This attack hit the starboard inner engine and light smoke began pouring from it. A second similar attack was made by the Japanese fighter five minutes later, but it scored no hits. A third attack was made, from above and head-on, and closed in to 150 yards, but, even though further hits were registered, the pilot could not shoot the B-24 down. During the attack, the Australian gunners opened fire, but without result. Their fire was enough to oblige the Japanese fighter to fly away, but it shadowed the Liberator for about fifteen minutes at a range of 4000 yards. The B-24 managed to return to base without major problems. On landing, damage to the propellers (engines 1 and 3) was noted, the starboard inner (engine 3) was losing oil, and the tail was holed in various places which resulted in a partial loss of elevator control. The encounter with the 'Oscar' was not to be a one-off occurrence and worse was to come. On 6 March, a new CO took over (S/L R.E. Bell). While the first three weeks of March were relatively uneventful with fifty sorties flown and all aircraft returning safely, the squadron now lost two Liberators in two days. On the 22nd, while on a search op, B-24 A72-59, captained exceptionally by the 82 Wing CO, G/C D.W. Kingwell, was attacked by two Japanese fighters, identified as a 'Zero' and an 'Oscar', in the vicinity of Bima. The Japanese scored various hits on the port bow of the Lib, wounding the nose gunner and the captain. The front turret was shot away and the hydraulic system damaged. Despite

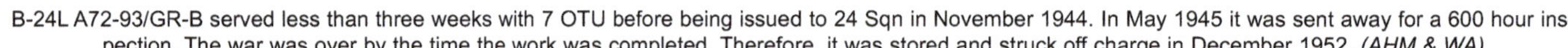

B-24L A72-93/GR-B served less than three weeks with 7 OTU before being issued to 24 Sqn in November 1944. In May 1945 it was sent away for a 600 hour inspection. The war was over by the time the work was completed. Therefore, it was stored and struck off charge in December 1952. *(AHM & WA)*

this, the B-24 managed to complete the homeward leg to base where it landed safely. Other damage was found in the rear fuselage, mainplanes, tailplanes and engine cowlings. The B-24 was declared unserviceable and sent for repairs which were never undertaken and A72-59 was eventually converted to components. The next day, four Liberators, led by S/L N.H. Straus, took off from Truscott strip for an armed shipping sweep. Straus was flying A72-80. The other B-24s were A72-77 (F/L E.V. Ford), A72-93 (F/L W.W. Kirkwood) and A72-67 (F/L R.McD. Beattie). Shortly after take off, S/L Straus called Truscott to indicate that he was preparing for an emergency landing. However, it became clear that, owing to his low altitude, S/L Straus could not locate the strip. For 23 minutes after take off the aircraft was airborne and, during this time, various messages from the aircraft were received by Truscott, and V.H.F. homing, and by the remainder of the aircraft in the formation. None of these messages referred to the exact cause of the distress as all that was heard was that the aircraft could not gain height. At 0713 hours, a message was received that S/L Straus was about to ditch in Vansittart Bay. Following this, the crews of the remaining three aircraft saw A72-80 ditch with wings level, but at a fairly high rate of descent. The B-24 caught fire on impact with the water and disintegrated. Only one body was recovered the same day, while two others, including Straus, were later found. The squadron would suffer greater loss two weeks later. On 6 April, it took part in the attack on the Japanese cruiser *Isuzu* north of Sumbawa with 21 Squadron. The first run was made over the Japanese cruiser and followed by a second ten minutes later. Some Japanese A6M 'Hamps' attacked the Liberators. The first to be hit was A72-81 (captained by F/O S.L. Macdonald) which sustained an attack from the ten o'clock position by two fighters. It seems that this attack was fatal as flames were seen coming from the cockpit area as the aircraft lost height. The bombs were jettisoned and the nose wheel compartment opened. Two members parachuted from the exit, while three more jumped from the bomb bay. The aircraft immediately climbed at a steep angle and appeared to reach the stall. Flames were then seen coming from the nose wheel compartment and forward of the bomb bay. The Liberator turned over on its left wing and plunged vertically towards the sea, losing about 6,000 feet. It recovered from the dive and went into a very steep climb and again stalled to the left and went into another dive of about 45° heading towards the cruiser. A few seconds later, the Liberator exploded. Then, A72-77 was attacked. A 'Hamp' made a head-on attack on the bomber, captained by F/L E.V. Ford, who was Number 3 of the third element, and hits were recorded on the starboard inner engine, while the gunners claimed the Japanese fighter as shot down after hits on the 'Hamp' were observed. The engine caught fire and flames were seen coming from near the Liberator's nose wheel. The B-24 was flying at 12,000 feet and the left wing was soon ablaze. The captain had no choice but to order the crew to abandon the aircraft. The back hatch was jettisoned and five men managed to jump as the aircraft was held level by Ford. However,

B-24J A72-40/GR-K returning from an op. Its first was recorded on 6 August 1944 and it would complete eleven more before being sent for a major inspection and re-issued to 7 OTU in late November 1944. It remained with the unit until the end of the war. *(AHM & WA)*

B-24M A72-179 'King Cobra' was allotted to 24 Sqn in April 1945. In July it was due for a 300 hour inspection and was then issued to 21 Sqn. *(AHM & WA)*

the Liberator then rolled over and, with Ford still at the controls, plunged into the sea where it exploded on impact. Of those who escaped from A72-77, only two survived, in addition to just one from A72-81. The Catalina that came to pick up the survivors of the two bombers was also attacked, causing more casualties, either killed by the Japanese fighters or drowned. A second Catalina picked up survivors, but had to abandon a search for more men as it was attacked by two 'Irvings'.

May was the quietest month in the squadron's history and only twenty sorties were flown. At the end of the month, the squadron began its deployment to Morotai where it was heavily employed in bombing sorties, alongside shipping reconnaissance flights, in preparation for the Balikpapan landings scheduled in July. More than 100 sorties were achieved in June. On 2 July, while on a co-operation exercise with the Army over Balikpapan, A72-64 was shot down by Japanese flak. All fourteen people on board perished. At first, the aircraft was posted missing and it remained so until information was received from a command ship that the Liberator had been hit by light anti-aircraft fire and had crashed into enemy held territory. The remains of the crew were discovered on 1 August. The next day, a B-24 (A72-184) was badly damaged on take off when the left wheel locked during the take off run, causing the aircraft to swing to the left and hit a bank at edge of the strip. Severe damage was done to the nose section and the aircraft was not repaired before the end of war. The flight had been scheduled to check out the co-pilot with a series of circuits and landings. Two days later, the squadron lost another B-24 (A72-196) to ground fire during a strike on Limboeng. The bomber was hit by light flak while flying at 200 feet. The starboard inner engine caught fire and the aircraft exploded, leaving no chance of survival for the crew. This was last loss sustained by 24 Squadron. That month, it completed about 100 sorties and followed them with about 35 more before VJ-Day was announced. The last offensive op was flown on the 12th to make a total of 750 sorties flown since conversion to the Liberator. After VJ-Day, the squadron remained active ferrying prisoners of war, tour-expired personnel and wounded patients back to Australia for discharge and rehabilitation, the peak of activity being reached in November with 1600 hours logged. The squadron then returned to Tocumwal where it was disbanded on 15 May 1946.

Claims - 24 Squadron RAAF (Confirmed and Probable)

Date	Capt of the crew	SN	Origin	Type	Serial	Code	Nb	Cat.
06.04.45	F/L Eric V. **Ford**	Aus. 255138	RAAF	'Hamp'	**A72-77**		1.0	C

Total: 1.0

Date	Crew	S/N	Origin	Serial	Code	Fate
07.09.44	F/L Cecil E.R. **Parsons**	Aus. 400419	RAAF	**A72-39**	GR-J	-
	Rest of tne crew unknown but safe					
23.01.45	P/O Kenwyn H. **Richards**	Aus. 407253	RAAF	**A72-70**		†
	W/O Evelyn B. **Baile**	Aus. 415603	RAAF			†
	W/O Leonard K. **Teitzel**	Aus. 405430	RAAF			†
	F/L Thomas G. **Evans**	Aus. 401186	RAAF			†
	Sgt Graham N. **Head**	Aus. 431625	RAAF			†
	Sgt Jack **Holt**	Aus. 412142	RAAF			†
	Sgt William J. **Cornes**	Aus. 435651	RAAF			†
	Sgt Noel P. **Martin**	Aus. 433734	RAAF			†
	F/L Kenneth W. **Edwards**	Aus. 400053	RAAF			†
	Sgt Joseph A.W. **Stevenson**	Aus. 425068	RAAF			†
	Sgt David K. **Kyle-Little**	Aus. 6584	RAAF			†
02.02.45	F/L Arthur A. **Cambridge**	Aus. 406750	RAAF	**A72-88**		-
	W/O Frederick **Crawford**	Aus. 425611	RAAF			-
	F/O Ivan F. **Coward**	Aus. 416415	RAAF			-
	F/L John R. **Parkinson**	Aus. 411371	RAAF			†
	P/O Geoffrey W. **Rhodes**	Aus. 413253	RAAF			-
	P/O Geoffrey N. **Johnson**	Aus. 416767	RAAF			-
	F/L Victor C.E. **Scanlon**	Aus. 416131	RAAF			-
	F/O John McP. **Pitt**	Aus. 401830	RAAF			†
	Sgt Ernest W. **Jennings**	Aus. 443957	RAAF			-
	F/Sgt Eric G.T. **Riley**	Aus. 411522	RAAF			-
	Sgt Ernest L. **Francis**	Aus. 442341	RAAF			-
	Sgt Allen G. **Cullen**	Aus. 19835	RAAF			-
22.03.45	G/C Deryck W. **Kingwell**	Aus. 138	RAAF	**A72-59**	GR-G	-
	F/O Kelvin A.R. **Brown**	Aus. 426804	RAAF			-
	S/L Stanley J. **Nichol**	Aus. 3485	RAAF			-
	F/O Alexander G. **Worley**	Aus. 435236	RAAF			-
	F/L Trevor C. **Lee**	Aus. 7208	RAAF			-
	W/O Keith R. **Shilling**	Aus. 406816	RAAF			-
	F/Sgt John S. **Thomson**	Aus. 438719	RAAF			-
	F/Sgt Ronald J. **Banks**	Aus. 436999	RAAF			-
	F/Sgt Trevor E. **Bowen**	Aus. 439863	RAAF			-
	F/Sgt Allan **Davis**	Aus. 431280	RAAF			-
	Sgt Walter J. **Wignall**	Aus. 17299	RAAF			-
	S/L Nathaniel H. **Straus**	Aus. 250759	RAAF	**A72-80**		†
	F/L Charles D. **Parry-Okeden**	Aus. 404485	RAAF			†
	F/O Raymond A. **Whiting**	Aus. 426733	RAAF			†
	F/O John W. **Hursthouse**	Aus. 416215	RAAF			†
	F/Sgt Harry J. **Boyd**	Aus. 427775	RAAF			†
	W/O William R. **Flanagan**	Aus. 401748	RAAF			†
	W/O Herbert G. **Parker**	Aus. 408591	RAAF			†
	F/Sgt John R. **Ryan**	Aus. 422716	RAAF			†
	F/Sgt William A.J. **Rodgers**	Aus. 436889	RAAF			†
	Sgt Alexander D. **Whitehead**	Aus. 121592	RAAF			†
	F/Sgt Ronald M. **Morris**	Aus. 46563	RAAF			†
	Cpl Douglas W. **Madden**	Aus. 36484	RAAF			†

Date	Name	Number	Service	Aircraft	Code	
06.04.45	F/O Sidney L. **McDonald**	Aus. 411524	RAAF	**A72-81**	GR-T	†
	P/O Keith A.R. **Brown**	Aus. 426804	RAAF			†
	F/O Peter A. **Mouatt**	Aus. 405523	RAAF			†
	F/O Alexander G. **Worley**	Aus. 435236	RAAF			†
	W/O Keith R. **Shilling**	Aus. 406816	RAAF			-
	F/Sgt Leslie K. **Walmsley**	Aus. 435740	RAAF			†
	F/Sgt John S. **Thomson**	Aus. 438719	RAAF			†
	F/Sgt Ronald J. **Banks**	Aus. 436999	RAAF			†
	F/Sgt Trevos E. **Bowen**	Aus. 439863	RAAF			†
	F/Sgt Allan **Davis**	Aus. 431280	RAAF			†
	Sgt Walter J. **Wingnall**	Aus. 17299	RAAF			†
	F/L Eric V. **Ford**	Aus. 255138	RAAF	**A72-77**		†
	W/O Colin G. **Vickers**	Aus. 401867	RAAF			-
	F/L Lance D. **Crowther**	Aus. 403560	RAAF			†
	F/L William **Laing**	Aus. 406568	RAAF			†
	F/O Bernard T. **Jordan**	Aus. 407825	RAAF			†
	W/O Alan N. **Collins**	Aus. 424373	RAAF			†
	F/Sgt Keith J. **White**	Aus. 433632	RAAF			†
	F/Sgt Leslie **Raine**	Aus. 439612	RAAF			†
	F/Sgt John M. **Waddell**	Aus. 443444	RAAF			†
	F/Sgt Ian **Faichnie**	Aus. 431408	RAAF			†
	Sgt William W.T. **Sayer**	Aus. 30337	RAAF			-
02.07.45	F/L Roy McD. **Beattie**	Aus. 404228	RAAF	**A72-64**		†
	F/L Athol M. **Andrews**	Aus. 412351	RAAF			†
	F/L Douglas W. **Willett**	Aus. 404424	RAAF			†
	F/L Harry **Stroud**	Aus. 403768	RAAF			†
	F/L Thomas **Hockings**	Aus. 425936	RAAF			†
	F/Sgt Denis G. **Featherstone**	Aus. 438726	RAAF			†
	F/Sgt Leonard R. **Sapwell**	Aus. 116599	RAAF			†
	F/Sgt Leslie W. **Devereux**	Aus. 438586	RAAF			†
	F/Sgt Arthur J. **Hogg**	Aus. 430751	RAAF			†
	F/Sgt Keith L. **Patten**	Aus. 440006	RAAF			†
	Cpl Ronald W.B. **Robinson**	Aus. 14526	RAAF			†
	and two Army personnel as passengers (†)					
05.07.45	S/L John R.W. **Redman**	Aus. 402395	RAAF	**A72-196**		†
	F/L Rex V. **Skinner**	Aus. 407185	RAAF			†
	W/O Harold A. **Gooding**	Aus. 418040	RAAF			†
	F/Sgt Martin A. **Burrows**	Aus. 12720	RAAF			†
	F/Sgt James O.R. **Vickers**	Aus. 66185	RAAF			†
	F/Sgt Ronald M. **Cornelious**	Aus. 436789	RAAF			†
	F/Sgt Roy **Tapper**	Aus. 434336	RAAF			†
	F/Sgt Leslie **Rogers**	Aus. 449787	RAAF			†
	F/Sgt Patrick F. **Stanley**	Aus. 430846	RAAF			†
	F/Sgt Harold **Shadforth**	Aus. 449303	RAAF			†
	F/Sgt Frederick L. **Rollings**	Aus. 438085	RAAF			†
	and one Army personnel as passenger (†)					

Total: 9

*Died in captivity.

Date	Crew	S/N	Origin	Serial	Code	Fate
02.07.45	F/L Arthur A. **CAMBRIDGE**	Aus. 406750	RAAF	**A72-184**		-
	F/O C. **WRIGHT**	Aus. ?	RAAF			-

Total: 1

Wearing 24 Squadron's codes, A72-99 still carries 23 Sqn tail markings. This B-24L was passed to 24 Sqn in October 1945 and served with that unit until it disbanded. *(AHM & WA)*

No. 12 Squadron RAAF (code NH)

A former Vengeance squadron that had operated in New Guinea, No. 12 Squadron RAAF had been reduced to a cadre unit by the end of 1944 when it began to receive its first Liberators. For that, it moved to Cecil Plains, near Dalby in Queensland, in December. New personnel and equipment arrived in January 1945, but the re-establishment of the squadron was slow as at the end of the month only six officers and ninety airmen were listed as being part of the squadron's strength. Aircraft had yet to be received, but the men were told they were to be allocated the B-24M. A new CO was appointed, W/C Neville G. Hemsworth, who arrived on 3 February, and the first B-24, A72-145, turned up three days later. Hemsworth was an experienced pilot who had flown Hudsons operationally in 1941 and 1942 and been shot down and severely burnt in the process. More personnel followed in February while A72-143, 160, 161, 163, 166, 167, 171, 173 and 188 were added to the inventory. Personnel strength reached 586 by the end of February. In March, the full complement of aircraft (A72-148 and 158 were the last two) and equipment was achieved and training was carried out until the end of April without major incident. The squadron was then relocated to Darwin. In May, the unit began operations attached to 21 Squadron to gain some operational experience. A dramatic accident occurred on 20 May when Liberator A72-160, taking off at night from Truscott airstrip, crashed. It was seen to veer left, shortly after take off, moving rather slowly and gaining little speed or height. The Liberator climbed to about 40 feet and then fell sharply to the ground. The fire crews rushed to the aircraft, but a number of the depth charges the aircraft was carrying exploded which left little chance of survival for the nine crewmen on board. This was the first major accident since conversion to the B-24. Nonetheless, operations began four days later on the 24th with two search missions, the first by A72-188 (S/L J.F. Murphy and crew), and the second by A72-158 (F/L V.E. Fitcher and crew), carried out. The latter found a motorboat that was strafed from 500 feet and sunk. Ten other search missions were flown before the end of the month – the 'Able' (anti-clockwise) and 'Baker' circuits (clockwise). The first three weeks of June saw the same kind of sortie carried out and various targets attacked, like huts or little crafts, with guns and bombs. On 21 June, the first strike was carried out. Led by the CO, the target was Ambesia airstrip, but the bombs fell 20-100 yards north of the strip. The same target was also bombed by three of the squadron's B-24s, led by S/L R.R. Russell, three days later, but as an alternative to the primary target, Kendari, because of a 10/10 cloud layer over the latter. Cloud was also responsible for the failure of the next strike on 25 June and only F/L A.J. Jamieson was able to drop his bombs on Timowo strip, the secondary target, with no result. The same misadventure happened on the 27th, the weather preventing any attack, and the G/C P.A. Parker (temporary OC of 82 Wing), who was leading, returned to base with all of his bombs. At last, a near successful strike was recorded on the 29th with half of the bombs falling on the strip at Ambesia. At the same time, the squadron began to exchange its B-24Ms for late batch B-24Js in the A72-300 sequence, a process that was completed by the end of the month. The number of operational flights dropped to less than fifty in July. However, the ratio of strikes against Japanese infrastructure increased, mainly Ambesia strip again, with poor results and little damage inflicted, while the rest of the sorties involved search missions during which A72-314, flown by S/L R.R. Russell and his crew, received four hits from 20mm anti-aircraft fire on the 29th. The Liberator was damaged enough to be sent off for repairs, but these were not completed by the end of war so the B-24 was converted to components in September. Two days later, the squadron had six Liberators airborne for another strike, the first time six aircraft were involved in such an op. That month, the squadron became part of No. 85 Wing RAAF alongside 99 Squadron (now also flying Liberators). On 1 August, S/L J.F. Murphy, one of the flight commanders, was appointed OC of the squadron as W/C Hemsworth departed to be discharged. The last strike, on a Japanese position during which ten large and sixteen smaller buildings and huts were destroyed, took place on 5 August. The final offensive sortie was carried out on the 10th when barracks at Kendari were bombed by F/L A.J. Jamieson. Four days later, an ASR mission for a missing B-25 (another ASR mission took place a week later) was flown by two Liberators, but the war was technically over with the surrender of the Japanese. The squadron was now charged with dropping leaflets, the last flights being recorded on the 22nd. If the leaflet drops are included, the squadron flew 152 sorties on the B-24. A new role was waiting for 12 as it was to be involved in transport, including the repatriation of ex-PoWs. The Liberators were progressively stripped of their armour plate and unnecessary equipment. Command of the squadron passed to S/L J.E.S Dennett in February 1946 and then to W/C J.B. Hampshire in August. He was still in

B-24J A72-322 wearing 12 Squadron's 'NH' code, but still without its individual letter. It was issued to the squadron in June 1945 and entered storage the following October. *(AHM & WA)*

command when the squadron converted to the Lincoln in June 1947. During that lapse of time, only one Liberator was written-off when A72-317 suffered an engine fire on take off on 23 September 1945. Fortunately, the crew escaped unscathed. However, as many B-24s were held in the depots, the aircraft was not repaired and was converted to components in October.

Summary of the aircraft lost on Operations - 12 Squadron RAAF

Date	Crew	S/N	Origin	Serial	Code	Fate
20.05.45	F/L Francis L. **SISMEY**	AUS. 402764	RAAF	**A72-160**		†
	F/O William S. **BELL**	AUS. 417693	RAAF			†
	W/O Thomas N. **RUST**	AUS. 408378	RAAF			†
	W/O Bernard L. **COX**	AUS. 412402	RAAF			†
	F/Sgt Leonard **DUCANSON**	AUS. 59752	RAAF			†
	F/Sgt Lester M. **BAILEY**	AUS. 443477	RAAF			†
	F/Sgt Ian N.L. **EASTON**	AUS. 439751	RAAF			†
	F/Sgt Thomas W. **ALLEN**	AUS. 440166	RAAF			†
	F/Sgt Donald D. **BENSON**	AUS. 435604	RAAF			†
	F/Sgt John A. **HOLLIS**	AUS. 445226	RAAF			†
	F/Sgt John R.W. **HERPS**	AUS. 440858	RAAF			†
30.07.45	S/L Robert R. **RUSSELL**	AUS. 270832	RAAF	**A72-314**		-
	Rest of tge crew not reported but safe					-

Total: 2

No. 21 Squadron RAAF (code MJ)

A Vengeance squadron operating in New Guinea, No. 21 Squadron was recalled to Australia in mid-1944 to be reformed as a heavy bomber squadron. It was sent to Leyburn in Queensland to undertake the conversion and was the second squadron to do so. The conversion began in early September, first with the arrival of a new CO, W/C (but soon G/C) P.A. Parker, who had flown Hudsons in Malaya in 1941 with No. 8 Squadron. He officially took command on the 7th. Over the following days, notifications were received of the imminent arrival of Liberators A72-52, 53, 55, 56, 60, 61, 64, 69, 71, 72, but the first to be delivered, A72-55, was only ferried in on 25 September. The rest arrived over the following weeks, well into October, with A72-58 and 68 arriving to compete the expected establishment. Training started at once, the build up continuing until the end of the year, with 165 hours logged in November and 86 in December. The squadron moved to Fenton, to be placed under 82 Wing's authority, at the end of the year. The first sorties, two armed reconnaissance flights around the islands to the west of Timor, were flown by S/L I.O. Black and crew in A72-53 and F/L T.L. Duigan and crew in A72-55 on 10 January. Both proved uneventful. The rest of the month was busy with 45 sorties flown. All were either anti-shipping searches or harassing raids over the Kendari-Ambesia area. While operations continued, work on the campsite had almost reached completion by the end of the month. In February the rhythm of sorties repeated those of January and the nature of the ops remained unchanged. On return, except in a few cases, little effective action was reported that month. On the 7th, while returning home after an uneventful search, A72-71, captained by F/L H.S. McDouall, experienced moderate, medium and heavy flak over Bima at 6000 feet. The B-24 was holed in several places, especially the tail. The rear gunner, F/O J. Doran, was injured and admitted to hospital on return to Darwin. Two days earlier, A72-68 had a misadventure on take off and overran the runway, fortunately without any consequences for the crew or major repairs for the B-24. During the month, two ops were also carried out from Truscott, the personnel arriving there the day before the strike. In March, 65 sorties were carried out, some from Truscott again, during which one major event occurred. While attacking a vessel on 17 March, the co-pilot of A72-68, F/O L.P. Roberts, was struck by shrapnel. One very accurate shot from heavy MGs hit the bombardier's compartment and severely damaged some electrical leads, hydraulic lines and the instrument panel. The elevator control chain in the second pilot's control column was also hit, injuring the co-pilot at the same time. The port inner engine had to be shut down. The captain of the B-24, F/L R.M. Hirst, was able to return to base and, fortunately, the wounds sustained by Roberts were not that serious as he was treated at the base by the Squadron Medical Section. The following day, A72-72 was also hit by flak while attacking another light Japanese installation, but this time no casualty was reported. That happened while on a low altitude run (200 feet). One bullet made a hole in the co-pilot's panel window while another hole was later found in the left wheel nacelle. When operating from Truscott, 21 was acting as a 'proper' heavy bomber squadron, dispatching formation boxes against ground targets, such as on 1 March when six aircraft bombed the Banjoewangi oil installations. Another conventional bombing strike was performed on the 12th against the Mapin barge staging point. At the end of the month, the CO, G/C Parker, was temporarily assigned to 85 Wing HQ, a position he would retain until the end of May. In all, including non-operational flights, 21 was proud to have flown close to 1000 hours of which 780 were operational. In April, it was decided that a detachment of personnel from 82 Wing would proceed to Morotai to carry out operations from that location under the direction of 1 TAF. The personnel comprising this detachment were drawn from 82 Wing Headquarters, 21 Squadron, 24 Squadron and 6 Repair and Servicing Unit. The move for 21 Squadron's personnel took place over several days during the month and the CO, G/C Parker, left on the 27th. As far as 21 was concerned, an average of eight B-24s was detached to Morotai in April. To avoid leaving the unit without an operational CO, command was given to G/C D. McLean. Air activity was maintained that month, more or less equally split between Morotai and Fenton. From Fenton, the sorties still mostly consisted of harassing shipping or attacking the airstrips at Kendari and Ambesia. On 4 April, F/L B.P. Butler and crew in A72-101 flew a night op. The Japanese lit six searchlights and dispatched a night fighter, but no shots were exchanged. On 6 April, the squadron, led by G/C Parker, participated, with 24 Squadron, in a raid against a Japanese convoy, four B-24s being engaged. Several attacks were made from 10,000 feet and heavy and accurate flak encountered. The squadron was lucky as 24 Squadron lost two B-24s during that raid, including one to Japanese 'Oscar' fighters. The unit's B-24s were also attacked by the Japanese fighters, and S/L G.J. White and crew in A72-56 claimed one as destroyed as it was seen to crash into the sea after being hit several times. In return, A72-56 was holed in various places by the fighter and added flak hits to the damage for good measure. None of the damage was, however, severe and no one on board was injured.

Morotai was to be used for the Allied attack on the Philippines, starting from the second week of April. The Americans asked, rather optimistically, that 800 hours per squadron be flown for the remaining 21 days of the month. The first raid was carried out on 13 April when three aircraft from the squadron (with three more from 24) attacked personnel infrastructure at Tawao in the north-east of Borneo. By the end of the month, six more targets were attacked.

On 1 May, another Liberator was damaged by ground fire, A72-108 captained by G/C Parker, but without any casualties fortunately. The aircraft and crew were part of the Morotai detachment. Parker returned to Fenton with his crew on 18 May, but it would be a short stay for him as he was finally posted to 85 Wing as OC and command of the squadron was given to G/C Don McLean. At the end of the month, notification was received that the squadron would move to an unspecified location as a component of 82 Wing. In the meantime, operations continued and a total of 117 operational hours were flown from Fenton, 166 more by the Morotai detachment. During the month, the squadron was reinforced by aircraft and crews from 12 Squadron and, under 21's authority, some anti-shipping sorties were flown. On 20 May, an accident caused the loss of a B-24 and the entire crew (see 12 Sqn text).

Early in June, 21 was fully involved in the last stages of the preparation for movement off the mainland. The air echelon, comprising four aircraft and crews together with 40 maintenance personnel, departed for Darwin. Five days later, the first element of the main party left Fenton to be embarked, the rest following over the next few days, with arrival at Morotai scheduled for the end of the month.

B-24J A72-56 served with 21 Sqn between September 1944 and July 1945 when it was sent to storage. It completed 23 operational sorties. *(AHM & WA)*

Another view of A72-56 as it prepares for take off from Piote Strip at Morotai.

On 19 June, G/C McLean was posted to 82 Wing HQ, relinquishing command to the B Flight CO, S/L I.O. Black. Operations continued from Morotai. Ground targets were the focus and these were attacked using conventional bombing runs. Three B-24s were normally dispatched to deal with a target. Around 100 sorties were carried out in June. On the first day of July, seven B-24s, led by S/L Black, participated in a strike on Balikpapan. An additional aircraft, A72-61, captained by the OC 82 Wing, G/C McLean, was flying with the squadron and one of its crew. The B-24 was hit by light AA and MacLean ordered the crew to abandon the aircraft. Not all could do so, and four, including McLean, were posted missing believed killed. Among the airmen lost was F/L J.A. Roy, the squadron's intelligence officer, who was acting as an observer. The remaining crew parachuted safely into the sea where they were later picked up. The squadron participated in about 25 bombing ops in July. On 27 July, A72-92 was sent for a reconnaissance mission over the Celebes to search alternative targets. Near Tomohoan, the B-24 was hit by anti-aircraft fire and failed to return. Four crew members were seen to bail out, the rest of the crew perished in the crash. The four crewmen who baled out were Sgt A.A. Lockyer, W/O G.G. Lindley, F/Sgt J.V. Orgill and F/Sgt C.N. Nichol. Tragically, Nichol bailed out without a parachute and died on impact. The other three Lockyer, Lindley,

B-24L A72-108 was provided to 21 Sqn as a replacement aircraft in December 1944 and put into action in April 1945. On 1 May it was damaged by enemy action (wing, undercarriage and port outer engine), but was soon repaired. It continued to be part of 21 Squadron's inventory until February 1946. *(AHM & WA)*

B-24M A72-179 just after it was transferred from 24 Sqn to 21 Sqn in August 1945. It still wears its previous owner's tail markings, but new codes, 'MJ-V', have already been added (see also the photo of this aircraft in 24 Sqn markings). *(AHM & WA)*

Orgill landed safely. Orgill landed in the garden of a Chinese family who attempted to persuade him to escape before the Japanese arrived. He refused until he could ascertain the fate of his comrades and was captured. Lockyer, Lindley, Orgill were captured by the Japanese and became PoWs. It was later reported by a native soldier reported that on arrival at the prison, Orgill grabbed the native soldier's bayonet and began attacking guards. Four Japanese soldiers subdued him and he was beaten with sticks for half an hour until unconscious. He was stripped of his clothing and thrown into a cell with Lindley and Lockyer, dying during the night. Warrant Officer Lindley and Sgt Lockyer, who had both been injured when baling out of the aircraft, were subject to brutal interrogations. On about August 5, they were moved to Kaaten and kept in solitary confinement. After midnight on August 21, both Lindley and Lockyer were moved from their cell to a garage where a grave had been dug. The first man was chloroformed and buried alive. The second was chloroformed but did not lose consciousness, so he was strangled with a piece of rope and then buried. A third B-24 was lost in action that month, four days later. During a raid against the Halmaheras led by S/L A.M. Greenfield, where 21 provided three B-24s (A72-94, 66 and 72), on 31 July, A72-66, captained by F/O J.B. Faviell, did not return and the crew of ten men perished. In July 1945, so close to the end of war, the squadron had been badly hit with the loss of three B-24s in action when, to date, it had escaped major incidents. Operations continued until 12 August when all offensive operations were suspended following the two atomic bombs (even though the personnel of the squadron had heard of the bomb dropped over Nagasaki on the 9th). The last op was carried out by three B-24s (A72-68, 94 and 145), a bombing raid against personnel around Lake Patia and Lake Line. Led by F/L R.H. Nossiter, this marked a total of close to 500 operational sorties on Liberators since January. The squadron then entered a phase of uncertainty as to its new role, but, in the meantime, it was involved in dropping leaflets or escorting ships, eleven sorties of which were flown in the second half of August. It was not before early September that the squadron learned that its new role would be transporting goods and personnel, a task first performed from Morotai and then from Tocumwal in New South Wales from the end of October. They were busy as, for example, about 1000 hours were flown from Morotai in September alone. The squadron continued to fly Liberators until October when it was advised that the B-24s would be placed in storage and the squadron would re-equip with the Lincoln bomber.

Claims - 21 Squadron RAAF (Confirmed and Probable)

Date	Capt of the crew	SN	Origin	Type	Serial	Code	Nb	Cat.
05.04.45	S/L Gilford J. **WHITE**	AUS. 280541	RAAF	'Oscar'	**A72-56**		1.0	C

Total: 1.0

Date	Crew	S/N	Origin	Serial	Code	Fate
01.07.45	G/C Donald **McLean**	Aus. 78	RAAF	**A72-61**	MJ-P	†
	F/L John A. **Roy**	Aus. 266200	RAAF			†
	P/O George **Cobban**	Aus. 422422	RAAF			-
	F/O Roy E. **Percival**	Aus. 431030	RAAF			-
	W/O Harley R. **Bardwell**	Aus. 419950	RAAF			†
	F/Sgt Kenneth A. **Gibson**	Aus. 439649	RAAF			-
	W/OJeffrey B. **Franklin**	Aus. 412582	RAAF			-
	F/Sgt John J. **Stanley**	Aus. 12584	RAAF			-
	F/Sgt John H. **Gillman**	Aus. 116553	RAAF			-
	Sgt Dennis L. **Martin**	Aus. 8811	RAAF			†
	F/Sgt Alan J. **Stuart**	Aus. 438881	RAAF			-
27.07.45	F/L Kenneth J. **Hanson**	Aus. 403585	RAAF	**A72-92**	MJ-D	†
	W/O John J.O. **Hume**	Aus. 427095	RAAF			†
	W/O Alfred **Cook**	Aus. 419295	RAAF			†
	F/Sgt Charles N. **Nichol**	Aus. 440381	RAAF			†
	W/O George G. **Lindley****	Aus. 427712	RAAF			†
	F/Sgt John V. **Orgill***	Aus. 441469	RAAF			†
	Sgt Frank G.V. **Hutton**	Aus. 437421	RAAF			†
	F/Sgt William J. **Maxwell**	Aus. 435994	RAAF			†
	F/Sgt Bredan M. **Heslin**	Aus. 440787	RAAF			†
	F/Sgt Stephen P. **Cloake**	Aus. 441014	RAAF			†
	Sgt Arnold A. **Lockyer****	Aus. 80471	RAAF			†
31.07.45	F/O Jack B. **Faviell**	Aus. 403916	RAAF	**A72-66**		†
	P/O William J. **Stubbs**	Aus. 418199	RAAF			†
	Sgt Neville H. **Playford**	Aus. 439635	RAAF			†
	Sgt Ronald J. **Walker**	Aus. 439333	RAAF			†
	W/O Bruce V. **Paech**	Aus. 416188	RAAF			†
	Sgt Gordon M. **Scott**	Aus. 23277	RAAF			†
	F/O Douglas P. **Dewhurst**	Aus. 403780	RAAF			†
	F/Sgt Robert W. **Delahunt**	Aus. 439573	RAAF			†
	F/Sgt Aubrey E. **Burgess**	Aus. 443659	RAAF			†

Total: 3

* as a Pow 28.07.45
**as a PoW 21.08.45

Squadron Leader J.T. Finlayson and his crew when operational with 23 Sqn. Back row: S/L Finlayson, F/O E.H. East (W/Op), W/O E.L. Sperring (Nav), F/Sgt 'Ned' Ward (Eng), F/L E.J. McDowell (W/Op), Sgt D. Sieber (AG). Front row: F/L A.St.J. Underwood (AG), F/L R. Vine (2nd pilot), Sgt Kearney (AG), F/L K.J.A. Craig (BA).

No. 23 Squadron RAAF (code NV)

Number 23 Squadron was flying Vengeances when it was withdrawn from New Guinea pending re-equipment with the B-24. It was to be the third squadron to undertake its conversion to the B-24. By November 1944 the unit was at Leyburn when, in the middle of the month, with reduced manpower, it began to be re-formed as a heavy bomber unit. A new CO arrived, W/C R.A. Dunne, who had previously earned the DFC in 1942 against the Japanese while flying Hudsons over the Dutch East Indies. The first three Liberators, A72-96, 99 and 100 were taken on charge on 22 November, and were followed by A72-102 and 103 three days later. Training commenced slowly while more B-24s were added in December (A72-91, 94, 98, 104 and 107), but only three hours entirely dedicated to training were flown in December. The squadron had to wait until February 1945 to see its establishment of men and material fulfilled. As for the aircraft, A72-82 and 86 were added to the inventory. The squadron was now fully equipped with B-24Ls.

Early in April, 23 moved to Long Airfield, near Fenton in the Northern Territory, where it became operational. On the 7th, S/L J.W. Finlayson, OC B Flight, and crew carried out the first operational sortie, an anti-shipping search. Later that day, F/L J. St.Q. Barrett and crew were also airborne for an anti-shipping search and conducted the first squadron's attack with two strafing passes on a light troop vessel. Some strikes were seen on the vessel, but some accurate AA fire holed the B-24 in the mainplane, fuselage and tail unit, but without any major consequence. One more search sortie was flown (F/L J.F. Swain and crew in A72-102), but it proved uneventful. The rest of the month was made up of similar search ops, but, on the 27th, the squadron mounted its first true bombing raid. Led by the CO, the six Liberators (A72-82, 86, 91, 99, 100, 103) attacked Binkalapa to neutralise the strip there. On return, the operation was considered a success as all of the bombs fell in the target area. Two days later, another strike was planned to attack Ambesia aerodrome. The strike was led by S/L R.T. Cupper, but this time only 40% of the bombs fell on the strip. This was the last op of the month, and in all the squadron carried out 53 sorties in April representing 750 hours of operational flying and close to ninety hours of training. On the first day of May, 23 harassed various aerodromes such as Malang, Kendari, Boeloedowang and Limboeng, the attacks being made by pairs of aircraft. The rest of the month was spent on anti-shipping searches, but on 25 May six B-24s attacked the Japanese float base of Soemba in a failed attempt to destroy the ground installations there. On 2 June, four of the unit's B-24s, led by S/L D.F. Miller, were escorted by Spitfires to attack Cape Chater aerodrome in Timor. The raid was considered a total success and four Japanese aircraft were destroyed on the ground. This op was given much publicity in southern Australian newspapers with compliments to S/L D.F. Miller and the crews concerned (Flight Lieutenants C.T. Lister, L. Halliday and R.M. Baines). On 6 June, 23 Squadron began its move to a new location when six B-24s departed Long for Darwin with equipment and passengers. Over the next few days, these aircraft would fly strikes on northern Borneo, using Darwin and Morotai as bases. The most important raid during this time took place on 10 June. Led by the CO, seven Liberators departed for Morotai where a bash was to be carried out in conjunction with seven B-24s of Nos. 21 and 24 Squadrons. The strike was on Labuan island and proved an outstanding success with all bombs falling in the target area. This marked the start of a temporary move to Morotai to assist in the preparations for the invasion of Borneo. That month, 23 added four B-24Ms to its inventory (A72-167, 171, 173 and 188) to replace aircraft that had had to leave for major overhaul after six months of intense use. Liberator A72-49, a B-24J, also arrived. June ended with the 150th Liberator sortie.

On 1 July, the squadron participated in the support of the landings at Balikpapan with six B-24s led by W/C Dunne, while three others, headed by S/L J.W. Finlayson, were tasked with neutralising Kendari strip. This raid was considered accurate. At the same time, the squadron continued to put up some of its aircraft for regular anti-shipping search ops which, most of the time, proved uneventful, or

B-24J A72-362/NV-K being refueled. It was one of the new batch of B-24s taken on charge at the end of October 1945. *(AHM & WA)*

there was no clear result after targets were attacked. On 8 July, however, F/L J.St.Q. Baines, in A72-86, made several attacks on small craft and left one burning and another sunk. Baines and his crew sank another barge on the 24th while F/L L. Halliday claimed one more the same day and then claimed another the following 1 August. That was achieved via two bombing runs during which very accurate AA was encountered and the Lib severely rocked on two occasions. Operational activity reduced to fifteen individual anti-shipping searches and four attacks were performed against barges and small vessels. Each time the B-24 left the area with the barge, or small vessel, burning. This low operational activity was also caused by the scarcity of enemy targets remaining within the Liberators' operating range. The last offensive flight was flown on the 9th. An ASR mission was launched on the 14th for a missing Mitchell and S/L R.T. Cupper took off in A72-99, but, owing to engine trouble, had to return to base early. In all, the squadron flew 225 offensive missions once it became operational on Liberators. The next day, 15 August, the official surrender of Japan was announced and a two-day stand down was declared to celebrate the great event. The unit resumed operational flights in September, but the nature of the flights changed, obviously, being either leaflet drops or area surveillance to anticipate any aggressive reaction from remaining Japanese personnel. To hammer home whom the victors were, air cover was also provided on the 10th with eight B-24s showing the flag over Koepang. Then, from the 12th, the squadron began to concentrate on supply drops to Allied PoWs still in Japanese hands. Thirty-three flights were achieved in September, including an ASR sortie flown by the newly arrived A72-348. These sorties, along with the transport of personnel, continued into October as the number of personnel began to be seriously reduced by subsequent discharges from the RAAF. In November, the squadron, now totally absorbed by its transport duties, relocated to Tocumwal. On 2 November, A72-359 departed Morotai for Melbourne with nurses on board when it crashed, fortunately with no injuries to its 35 occupants. The aircraft caught fire and repairs were not even considered so the Liberator was converted to components. At the end of the month, 23 was operating eight B-24s (all in the 300 range and all B-24Js of the latest types) with 381 personnel, nearly half of the normal establishment. By April 1946, having been under the command of W/C J.E. Handbury since January, W/C Dunne's replacement, this work had largely been achieved and the squadron moved to Amberley where its conversion to the Lincoln began. Two days before the move, the squadron suffered a dramatic accident when it learned that A72-348, captained by the new CO, had ditched into the sea on the return flight from Japan. The B-24 was completing its leg from Manila to Darwin when problems with the two port engines were encountered and Handbury was forced to ditch. One man (F/L P.W. Matthews, the navigator), of the seven on board, was killed as was one of the two USN passengers. It was a sad way to end the squadron's association with the Liberator as it had avoided fatal losses since its conversion to the type. In May, conversion to the Lincoln was complete and 23 Squadron's time with the Liberator was officially at an end.

Date	Crew	S/N	Origin	Serial	Code	Fate
02.11.45	F/L Charles W. **BOYTON**	AUS. 402723	RAAF	**A72-359**		-
	W/O Philip A. **COACH**	AUS. 419928	RAAF			-
	F/Sgt Leonard **MURRAY**	AUS. 45265	RAAF			-
	F/L Albert W. **MARTIN**	AUS. 428730	RAAF			-
	35 pax, all safe					
09.04.46	W/C John E. **HANDURRY**	AUS. 395	RAAF	**A72-348**		-
	F/L Donald A. **WINCH**	AUS. 406226	RAAF			-
	F/L Philip W. **MATTHEWS**	AUS. 406080	RAAF			†
	F/Sgt Douglas W. **NORTON**	AUS. 39721	RAAF			-
	W/O Robert B. **SMITH**	AUS. 19667	RAAF			-
	W/O William N. **NESBITT**	AUS. 433943	RAAF			-
	W/O Colin J. **MacKENZIE**	AUS. 422241	RAAF			-
	Cpl Edgar E. **PYE**	AUS. 34387	RAAF			-

Total: 2

No. 25 Squadron RAAF (code SY)

Number 25 Squadron was the fourth RAAF unit to convert to the B-24. In the beginning of January 1945, major changes occurred to facilitate the transition with a move to Cunderdin (Western Australia) and the arrival of a new CO, W/C N.G. Hemsworth. His command would be short, however, as he was posted to command No. 12 Squadron before the end of January. Temporary command was given to S/L J.E. Dennett. During the month, more personnel arrived and the B-24s assigned were taken on charge. By the end of the month, A72-124, 133, 134, 137, 140, 144, 149, 150, 151, 152, 154 and 156 had been added to the inventory. The month was spent organising the squadron as a heavy bomber unit so less than 150 hours were flown. Nevertheless, 25 managed to get three B-24s and crews serviceable by the end of the month and sent three (A72-134 – S/L Dennett and 133 – F/L A.W. Archer, A72-149 – F/L R.J. Kavanagh) to Pearce to conduct anti-submarine patrols. The first was carried out on the 29th by A72-134 (Dennett). A second one was flown the next day by A72-149. These sorties were intensified in February with reinforcement from more B-24s after the sinking of the motor vessel Peter Silvester in the Indian Ocean some 800 miles from Fremantle, Western Australia. The squadron received a congratulatory message from the Air Staff with regard to its success in helping locate survivors. However, that came at a cost as, on taking off for one such search, A72-124 crashed shortly after it became airborne and caught fire on impact just 800 yards from the end of the runway. Five of the crew were killed, but the six other men escaped with slight shock and abrasions. Alongside the anti-submarine patrols, the squadron continued its training and two-thirds of the hours flown in February were dedicated to this task. This was achieved despite problems with the supply of some spare parts, the lack of which reduced the serviceability rates of the B-24s.

The first bombing sorties were carried out on 13 March from Fenton when six aircraft, led by S/L Dennett, participated in attacking a barge staging point in Timor. The raid was flown in conjunction with six B-24s from 21 Squadron. The strike was successful in that all bombs fell in the target area with excellent coverage. The last raid of the month took place on the 28th, a shipping sweep through Alas and Lombok Straits.

No operations were undertaken in the first three weeks of April, but, on 21 April, on return from an air test, A72-156 was held off a little too high as the power was pulled off. As the machine sank, the pilot pulled the stick back hard to decrease the sink rate. This caused the tail to drop sharply and the aircraft hit the ground with its tail skid which was destroyed on impact. No injuries were reported by the crew and the Liberator was eventually repaired to return to the squadron in July, but did not fly on operations again. Five days later, eight B-24s were detailed to attack Malang aerodrome on Java during the night of 26/27 April in order to prevent its use during the Allied landings at Tarakan. Bad weather obscured both Malang and the secondary target, Denpasar in Bali, and results of the attack could not be seen. On the return flight, the radio operator of A72-133 sent out a message that the aircraft was vibrating badly and they were making for Truscott. Nearly two hours later, another short message was received reporting that they were ditching. While Air Sea Rescue Catalinas and other Liberators soon located the site of the ditching off Soemba Island, no sign of the crew was seen. The B-24 was strafed by aircraft from several squadrons to destroy it, but the sea in the area was too shallow to cover the wreckage completely. As for the crew, they were eventually captured and all survived harsh Japanese captivity to return to Australia at the end of the war. The squadron spent the rest of the month harassing the same targets. That month, 25 encountered acute problems with spare parts'

B-24M A72-151/SJ-M served with 25 Sqn between January 1945 and April 1946. Stored, it was eventually struck off charge in December 1952. *(AHM & WA)*

shortages and was forced to strip parts from A72-134 to make A72-151 serviceable. No operations were carried out in May, the only event of interest being on 11 May when W/C J.B. Hampshire arrived to take command of the squadron from S/L J.E.S. Dennett who left a week later to command No. 102 Squadron as it formed on Liberators. At the end of the month, on the 30th, replacement B-24s for the lost A72-133 and A72-190 arrived. That helped to keep the squadron at a satisfactory level of serviceability (65%), but five of the aircraft were due for their 300 hour inspections at the end of the month so would not be available for June. That month, operations quietly resumed, with only twenty sorties recorded, and were followed by another 22 in July. The targets like Tandjeong Perak, Malang, or the ship building area at Semerang, were repeatedly visited. In August, two raids were carried out before VJ-Day, the first on the 3rd and another on the 5th, and marked the end of the squadron's time on offensive operations during which it completed less than 100 Liberator sorties.

From September 1945 to January 1946, the squadron was involved in the repatriation of Australian prisoners of war and internees from Borneo and Morotai to Australia. It was finally disbanded on 9 July 1946.

Summary of the aircraft lost on Operations - 25 Squadron RAAF

Date	Crew	S/N	Origin	Serial	Code	Fate
14.02.45	F/O Francis L. **Hannah**	Aus. 405177	RAAF	**A72-124**		-
	P/O Claremont L. **Taylor**	Aus. 405237	RAAF			-
	F/Sgt Francis G. **Coman**	Aus. 426953	RAAF			-
	F/Sgt Campbell E.E. **Verey**	Aus. 424238	RAAF			-
	F/Sgt Brian J.T. **Johnson**	Aus. 444015	RAAF			†
	Sgt Kenneth W. **Uhr**	Aus. 433831	RAAF			†
	Sgt Charles R. **Taylor**	Aus. 41804	RAAF			†
	Sgt George K. **Leroy**	Aus. 440793	RAAF			-
	Sgt Francis J. **Naughton**	Aus. 449767	RAAF			†
	Sgt Roy **Higginbottom**	Aus. 8503	RAAF			†
	Sgt Bernard **McTernan**	Aus. 426144	RAAF			-

26.04.45	S/L Jack A. **Wawn**	Aus. 261720	RAAF	**A72-133**	SJ-B	**PoW**
	F/L David W.J. **Buchanan**	Aus. 420132	RAAF			**PoW**
	F/O Colin C.A. **Robertson**	Aus. 412704	RAAF			**PoW**
	F/O Peter S. **Sykes**	Aus. 424228	RAAF			**PoW**
	F/L Lyndon L. **McKenzie**	Aus. 416284	RAAF			**PoW**
	F/O Ronald T. **Roberston**	Aus. 418680	RAAF			**PoW**
	F/Sgt Bernard W. **McInerney**	Aus. 438399	RAAF			**PoW**
	F/Sgt Norman W. **Haywood**	Aus. 115806	RAAF			**PoW**
	Sgt Desmond J. **Moloney**	Aus. 432724	RAAF			**PoW**
	W/O Thomas **Bonnice**	Aus. 401737	RAAF			**PoW**
	Sgt Lloyd F. **Medwin**	Aus. 29811	RAAF			**PoW**
	F/L Ernest R. **Oldfield**	Aus. 406221	RAAF			**PoW**

Total: 2

B-24M A72-150/SJ-L displaying the unique squadron tail marking, a black swan. Like A72-151, it flew with 25 Sqn until April 1946. *(AHM & WA)*

<u>**No. 99 Squadron RAAF (code UX)**</u>

Number 99 Squadron was formed at Leyburn (Queensland) on 1 February 1945 under the temporary command of S/L J.H. Marshall, a long-serving RAAF officer. Indeed Marshall enlisted at the outbreak of war as a regular officer and served with various RAAF Hudson squadrons during the first two years of the conflict. He served with 8 Squadron in Malaya before being evacuated to Australia in February 1942. Marshall spent a bit more time as an operational pilot, but from the summer of 1942 onwards he was posted to non-operational positions until December 1944 when he was posted to No. 23 Squadron. In March, 99 Squadron moved to Jondaryan where training continued. On 1 April, W/C A.E. Cross took over the squadron. He had served in the UK early in the war. That month, seven of the planned twelve B-24s were taken on charge and consisted of a mixed bag of B-24Ls (A72-141 and 153) and B-24Ms (A72-168, 178, 184, 194). In May, an advance party moved to Darwin to commence operations, but the process was somewhat leisurely as the move was still not complete in September. In May, the full complement of Liberators had been received and the disliked B-24Ms gone. The squadron's strength was now made up of mostly J-models (A72-300, 301, 302, 303, 304, 305, 306, 307, 308, 309, 311 and 313), while two B-24Ls (A72-141 and 153) were maintained. Following the end of the war, 99 Squadron operated in a transport role and was responsible for flying personnel and supplies between Darwin and southern Australia. One such flight marked the end of the career of A72-306 when, on 16 August, during the take off run from Amberley, the aircraft's brakes were applied before it was safely in the air. This caused the nose of the aircraft to strike the runway heavily, collapsing the nose wheel assembly and shearing hydraulic lines for the engine controls which then caused the aircraft to skid off the end of the runway and into a small ravine. Four of the crew on board were killed. The squadron suffered a second loss one month later on 14 September when a Liberator crashed near Amberley killing five more crewmembers. Transport operations continued throughout October, with the squadron's aircraft transporting around 800 passengers, most of whom were recently liberated Allied prisoners of war, and a large quantity of freight. In November, 99 Squadron moved from Darwin to Tocumwal, New South Wales. As the demobilisation process began, the squadron was slated for disbandment in March 1946, but the unit finally ceased to be on 5 June 1946.

Taken on charge by 99 Squadron in May 1945, B-24J A72-305 was coded UX-H. Note that this B-24 still has its US serial painted on the fin. When this photo was taken, A72-305 was serving in the transport role as can be seen by the lack of guns in the tail turret. *(AHM & WA)*

Date	Crew	S/N	Origin	Serial	Code	Fate
16.08.45	S/L William L. **Milne**	Aus. 616	RAAF	**A72-306**	UX-J	-
	W/O Eric F. **Carlson**	Aus. 424965	RAAF			†
	F/Sgt Jack G. **Watson**	Aus. 6571	RAAF			-
	F/Sgt Marcel K. **Doolan**	Aus. 439701	RAAF			-
	F/Sgt Arthur K. **Clausen**	Aus. 439868	RAAF			†
	F/Sgt Warwick M. **Lane**	Aus. 445024	RAAF			-
	F/Sgt Andrew K.C. **Cochrane**	Aus. 436739	RAAF			-
	F/Sgt Allan C. **Annetts**	Aus. 444988	RAAF			-
	2 of 11 passengers killed					
14.09.45	F/O Raymond F. **Pullin**	Aus. 411050	RAAF	**A72-313**		†
	F/L George A. **Hendy**	Aus. 401441	RAAF			†
	F/O James H. **Mutton**	Aus. 34046	RAAF			†
	Sgt George A. **Dureau**	Aus. 13926	RAAF			†
	F/Sgt Vincent J. **Quinn**	Aus. 437876	RAAF			†

Total: 2

Thanks to the US serial still painted on the fin (428139), this B-24 can be identified as A72-311. It belongs to the batch of B-24Js issued to 99 Squadron in May 1945. It is seen during a training flight in the summer of 1945 with all guns installed. *(AHM & WA)*

No. 102 Squadron RAAF (code BV)

Number 102 Squadron was the last RAAF Liberator unit to be formed. The date of formation was 30 May at Cecil Plains, Queensland. Command was given to S/L J.E.S. Dennett. In June, the squadron began to build up with the arrival of many personnel, but the first two B-24Js, A72-335 and A72-336, arrived on 5 July. More Liberators arrived soon after and ten were in the inventory by the end of July (A72-334, A72-337 to 340, A72-343 to A72-345 were the new arrivals). Early in August, the last two B-24Js, A72-341 and A72-342, were added, the latter being the final arrival on 12 August. Training was still underway when the war ended on the 15th. Despite this, flights continued and more than 350 hours were completed on Liberators which included participation in a mass formation over Brisbane on the 16th (102 contributed nine aircraft) to celebrate VJ-Day. During the last four months of 1945, aircraft and crews were kept busy operating from Amberley on ferry duties. The squadron eventually ceased all flying duties from 20 December 1945 onwards as the process of disbandment began. The final clap came on 18 March 1946 when the unit was officially disbanded.

B-24J A72-340/BV-G wearing full squadron markings at Cecil Plains in the summer of 1945. *(AHM & WA)*

No. 200 Flight (code NX)

Number 200 Flight was formed at Laverton on 15 February 1945 to conduct special duties operations. The flight was placed under the command of S/L H.G. Pockley who had served with No. 10 Squadron RAAF in Coastal Command in the UK. Interestingly, this unit was controlled by the Australian Intelligence Bureau (AIB). Formation was rapid and training had already begun by the end of the month with the first Liberators taken on (A72-182, A72-191, A72-192 and A72-159) and, when the flight became operational, A72-180 was added to the inventory. They were modified with their ball turrets and armour plate removed to reduce weight and extend operational range. In the same vein, ammunition capacity was reduced by 50%. A special slide chute for dropping paratroops was installed at the rear of the fuselage. The aircraft were also equipped with special radio-navigation equipment.

Because of the nature of the unit's tasks, to assist the clandestine operations of Australian Army personnel and their local supporters in Japanese-occupied North Borneo, Brunei and Sarawak, no details of the operations flown were required by RAAF Command in order to maintain as much secrecy as possible over the operations. Parachuting agents, and re-supplying them with stores and equipment, were the basic tasks requested of the flight. These ops could involve one to three Liberators and early flights were flown from the central Philippines. The first was carried out between 15 and 27 March, involving three B-24s, but had a bad outcome when, on the 25th, A72-191 and A72-159 carried out a SD (Special Duty) mission from which the former, with the CO on board, failed to return. Searches for the missing B-24 over the next few days proved fruitless. Pockley was replaced by W/C E.V. Read from mid-April. More sorties were given to the flight, the second op running from 9 to 20 April, and followed by the third between 15 April and 9 May. Two Liberators were lost in quick succession: A72-159 on the 17th was shot down near Vila General Carmona in Portuguese Timor while on its way to the forward base with five Army agents on board; and A72-177 hit a tree and crashed during a supply drop in Borneo on the 25th. The latter was part of the fourth mission. In both cases, the crews perished. The fifth operation, from 21 May to 8 June, was a single aircraft task involving supply drops flown from Puerto Princesa, by F/O F.A. Weir and his crew in A72-192, while the sixth ended on 13 July with the return of F/L L.G. Anderson and his crew in A72-183. In July, after six months of operations, the B-24s had to progressively start their 300 hour inspections. Another op was performed from 5 July with A72-185 (F/L D.A. Winch and crew). They carried out two sorties before returning to Leyburn. After two days off, they returned to operations in A72-183 on the 16th while W/C Read and his crew flew nine SD sorties in A72-187 during the month. Flight Lieutenant Wallace and his crew flew seven in A72-192. Operations continued after VJ Day, unlike most bomber units, and the work became even more varied with supply drops to Filipino paramilitary forces in Palawan and near Zamboanga (Mindanao), and also to Batavia. The flight was also tasked with 'normal' transport supply missions. The final supply drop was carried out on 26 September in A72-180 (F/L L.G. Anderson and crew). In all, about 100 SD sorties were carried out by the flight. It was then occupied with transport runs to evacuate remaining AIB personnel while the number of assigned personnel began to decline due discharges. When the recovery of all AIB personnel was completed, the days of the flight were numbered. Disbandment came on 15 December 1945.

Summary of the aircraft lost on Operations - 200 Flight RAAF

Date	Crew	S/N	Origin	Serial	Code	Fate
25.03.45	S/L Harold G. **Pockley**	Aus. 260608	RAAF	**A72-191**		†
	F/O Charles I. **Cox**	Aus. 415403	RAAF			†
	F/L Leonard F. **Day**	Aus. 409672	RAAF			†
	Sgt Leslie E. **Tonkin**	Aus. 443698	RAAF			†
	Sgt Kenneth C. **Wilmhurst**	Aus. 28787	RAAF			†
	F/L David P. **Gradwell**	Aus. 8960	RAAF			†
	Sgt Keith M. **Low**	Aus. 435733	RAAF			†
	Sgt Charles K. **Ponting**	Aus. 434348	RAAF			†
	F/O Ronald R. **Farmer**	Aus. 412503	RAAF			†
	Sgt Eric M. **Lichtfield**	Aus. 439370	RAAF			†
	Sgt Robert R. **Hale**	Aus. 444233	RAAF			†
	One British Army officer killed					
17.05.45	F/O Archibald M. **Clark**	Aus. 402309	RAAF	**A72-159**		†
	F/O Tom T. **Biltoft**	Aus. 404525	RAAF			†
	F/L Henry R. **Campbell**	Aus. 411860	RAAF			†
	F/O Colin M. **Manning**	Aus. 409282	RAAF			†
	F/L John W. **Rice**	Aus. 412186	RAAF			†
	F/O Herbert J. **Clark**	Aus. 413153	RAAF			†
	F/O Lionel J. **Brown**	Aus. 413536	RAAF			†
	F/O Herbert A.J. **Jones**	Aus. 411222	RAAF			†
	F/Sgt Clarence A.R. **Gamble**	Aus. 439646	RAAF			†
	Sgt Harry **Riley**	Aus. 14457	RAAF			†
	and 5 'Z' Special Force members killed					
21.05.45	F/L Keith R.N. **Emmett**	Aus. 411761	RAAF	**A72-177**		†
	F/O Ernest F. **Theyer**	Aus. 422755	RAAF			†
	F/L John O. **Graham**	Aus. 418101	RAAF			†
	P/O Reginald L. **Taylor**	Aus. 120044	RAAF			†
	F/O Rodney N. **Walker**	Aus. 421421	RAAF			†
	F/Sgt John C.W. **Anderson**	Aus. 424011	RAAF			†
	W/O Philip H. **Cormack**	Aus. 421295	RAAF			†
	F/Sgt Owen W.J. **Davern**	Aus. 5312	RAAF			†
	W/O Ernest T. **Shorter**	Aus. 14791	RAAF			†
	W/O Ralph **Proudlock**	Aus. 420488	RAAF			†
	Sgt Lawrence J. **Starr**	Aus. 71522	RAAF			†

Total: 3

B-24M A72-183/NX-R of 200 Flight undergoing some outdoor maintenance.

B-24M A72-186/LV-A at Laverton in 1945. 201 Flight did not become operational because of the time needed to fit the required radio equipment for operations. *(AHM & WA)*

No. 201 Flight (code LV)

This flight was formed as an electronic countermeasures unit at Laverton, Victoria, on 10 March 1945. The RAAF had recognised the need to be able to locate radar stations and jam radars that controlled searchlights. Temporary command was given to F/L K.R.N. Emmett until the appointed CO, W/C G.S. Davis, arrived on 20 March. This officer had served in the RAF early in the war in North Africa and was awarded the DFC while serving with No. 38 Squadron. The flight had an official establishment of six B-24 Liberators. On 27 March, two B-24Ms, A72-186 and A72-197, were allotted and while the former was delivered on 5 April, A72-192 was only received on the 27th. These aircraft still had to be fitted with appropriate radio equipment in specially modified radio compartments. Therefore, A72-186 was the first to go to No. 1 Aircraft Performance Unit (1 APU) at Laverton to undergo these changes. That month, various requested amendments, like a reduction in armourers, considering the nature of the tasks the flight would undertake, were approved. As bombing raids were not part of the flight's role, few of these men were needed, but, on the other hand, radar mechanics and other related personnel were needed in greater numbers. On 17 April, while only 60% of the equipment demanded had been received, the ground party began the move to Darwin. In May, various test flights were carried out with A72-186 at 1 APU. In June, the internal structural modifications were eventually approved and modifications to A72-197 could begin. However, as the two B-24Ms were often grounded, a third B-24, A72-357, a J-model, was requested by the CO to avoid any disruption in training the crews. It was delivered in August. By 30 June, work on A72-186 was almost complete except for the installation of the AN/APR-4 auto-scanning radar intercept receivers as they were still unavailable. So, AN/APR-1 equipment was installed instead. Flight tests were delayed by bad weather for several days and, when they resumed, it was found that the direction finding antenna was giving incorrect bearings. Eventually, only two training flights were performed between June and August when the AN/APR-4 equipment finally arrived.

The war against Japan was about to end when the unit was recalled to Ascot Vale near Melbourne. At that time, the flight's three B-24s received their code letters: LV-A (A72-186), LV-B (A72-197) and LV-D (A72-357). The code LV-C was reserved for a fourth B-24, A72-350 (J-model), but it was never received. Work was still underway on A72-197 when the war ended and the move of the remainder of the flight to Darwin was eventually abandoned. In the meantime, the final tests were carried out on A72-186 in September and proved successful with regard to soundproofing, even though additional ventilation was recommended. That same month discussions to retain or disband 201 Flight in the post-war RAAF got underway. At first it was decided not to disband the unit so, in October 1945, its headquarters moved to Laverton. However, on 18 December, a signal was received that the unit was to cease functioning from the 17th. The two ECM B-24s, A72-186 and A72-197, were allotted to No. 1 Aircraft Performance Unit (APU) on 28 February 1946, while A72-357 was ferried for storage by the CO himself on the 27th. Two weeks later, on 15 March 1946, the flight was disbanded.

OTHER ROLES

Aside from its operational usage, the RAAF used the B-24 in other roles. Three aircraft (A72-87, A72-198 and A72-315) were used at different times by 1 APU where they were used for various experiments until January 1947.

Some B-24s were also used as VIP aircraft, but only two completed their full careers in the RAAF as VIP transport aircraft. The first was A72-172, which was converted as early as March 1945, and it eventually served with No. 1 Communication Unit and 82 Wing HQ until September 1948. Liberators A72-189 and A72-193 had a similar career with the RAAF. The latter also made the last recorded flight of a B-24 in RAAF service on 21 January 1949.

*Returned to 5th AF
#Did not return from its last mission
In brackets Aircraft on loan

Serials and main units		Type	Formerly	Known mission tally
A72-1:	7 OTU	B-24D-CO	41-11904	-
A72-2:	7 OTU	B-24D-1-CO	41-23720	-
A72-3:	*Instructional airframe*	B-24D-15-CO	41-24018	-
A72-4:	7 OTU	B-24D-65-CO	42-40489	-
A72-5:	7 OTU	B-24D-65-CO	42-40512	-
A72-6:	*Instructional airframe*	B-24D-65-CO	42-40522	-
A72-7:	*Instructional airframe*	B-24D-15-CO	41-24070	-
A72-8:	7 OTU	B-24D-25-CO	41-24290	-
A72-9:	7 OTU	B-24D-CO	41-11868	-

B-24D A72-9, named 'White Cargo', while with 1 AD and used for test pilot training and ferry flights. Note the nose has been covered with metal plates. Its previous identity was 'Change O' Luck' with the 320th BS, 90th BG. This photo was taken at Tocumwal after the war. *(AHM & WA)*

B-24D A72-10 still in its USAAF camouflage and 'Rio Rita' noseart. It was withdrawn from use and stored in October 1944 after being damaged in a hangar fire. *(AHM & WA)*

A72-10:	7 OTU	B-24D-20-CO	41-24127	-
A72-11:	7 OTU	B-24D-65-CO	42-40514	-

A former 529th BS, 380th BG USAAF machine named 'Lucky', A72-11 served with 7 OTU between September 1944 until 22 April 1945 when it was damaged in a forced landing at Cooktown. *(AHM & WA)*

A72-12: 7 OTU	B-24D-135-CO	42-41132	-*
A72-13: 7 OTU	B-24J-80-CO	42-100194	-*
A72-14 to A72-30 not allocated			
A72-31: 24 *[GR-A]*, 7 OTU	B-24J-155-CO	44-40251	**20**
A72-32: 24 *[GR-B]*, 7 OTU	B-24J-155-CO	44-40252	**11**
A72-33: 7 OTU	B-24J-160-CO	44-40410	-
A72-34: 24 *[GR-D]*, 7 OTU	B-24J-160-CO	44-40406	**11**
A72-35: 24, 7 OTU	B-24J-160-CO	44-40408	**23**
A72-36: 7 OTU	B-24J-160-CO	44-40409	-
A72-37: 24, 7 OTU	B-24J-160-CO	44-40407	**17**
A72-38: 24 *[GR-G]*, 7 OTU	B-24J-160-CO	44-40411	**24**
A72-39: 24 *[GR-J]*	B-24J-175-CO	44-40653	**7#**
A72-40: 24 *[GR-K]*, 7 OTU	B-24J-175-CO	44-40649	**12**
A72-41: 24, 7 OTU	B-24J-175-CO	44-40652	**2**
A72-42: 24 *[GR-M]*, 7 OTU	B-24J-175-CO	44-40651	**10**
A72-43: 24, 7 OTU, 23, 82 Wing, 24	B-24J-175-CO	44-40654	**9**
A72-44: 24 *[GR-H]*, 7 OTU	B-24J-175-CO	44-40650	**15**
A72-45: 7 OTU, 12	B-24J-185-CO	44-40870	-
A72-46: 7 OTU	B-24J-185-CO	44-40871	-
A72-47: 24 *[GR-P]*, 7 OTU	B-24J-185-CO	44-40872	**7**
A72-48: 24, 7 OTU, 23	B-24J-185-CO	44-40873	**9**

B-24J A72-47 was issued to 24 Sqn for a short time before being passed to 7 OTU in November 1944. It served there for over a year before being withdrawn from use in December 1945.

A72-49: 24, 21, (23), 21	B-24J-200-CO	44-41194	**22**
A72-50: 7 OTU	B-24J-200-CO	44-41197	-
A72-51: 7 OTU	B-24J-200-CO	44-41203	-
A72-52: 21, 24, 21	B-24J-200-CO	44-41207	**22**

B-24J A72-51 spent all of its Australian career training crews at 7 OTU between September 1944 and the disbandment of the unit. *(AHM & WA)*

A72-53: 21, 23	B-24J-200-CO	44-41203	**22**
A72-54: 24 *[GR-K]*	B-24J-200-CO	44-41196	**22**
A72-55: 21, 24, 21	B-24J-200-CO	44-41206	**32**
A72-56: 21 *[MJ-W]*, (24), 21	B-24J-200-CO	44-41193	**25**
A72-57: 24, 21	B-24J-200-CO	44-41205	**32**
A72-58: 21 *[MJ-E]*, (24), 21	B-24J-200-CO	44-41195	**25**
A72-59: 7 OTU, 24 *[GR-G]*	B-24J-210-CO	44-41389	**17#**
A72-60: 21 *[MJ-V]*	B-24J-210-CO	44-41388	**22**
A72-61: 21 *[MJ-P]*	B-24J-210-CO	44-41375	**27#**
A72-62: 7 OTU	B-24J-205-CO	44-41249	-
A72-63: 7 OTU	B-24J-210-CO	44-41374	-
A72-64: 21, 24	B-24J-210-CO	44-41384	**26#**
A72-65: 7 OTU	B-24J-210-CO	44-41385	-
A72-66: 21	B-24J-210-CO	44-41373	**16#**
A72-67: 7 OTU, 24 *[GR-O]*	B-24J-210-CO	44-41386	**33**
A72-68: 21 *[MJ-O]*	B-24J-210-CO	44-41376	**20**
A72-69: 21 *[MJ-H]*	B-24L-1-CO	44-41391	**29**
A72-70: 7 OTU, 24	B-24L-1-CO	44-41392	**7**
A72-71: 21 *[MJ-F]*, (24), 21	B-24L-1-CO	44-41393	**29**
A72-72: 21, (24), 21	B-24L-1-CO	44-41394	**27**
A72-73: 7 OTU, 24	B-24L-1-CO	44-41401	**30**
A72-74: 7 OTU, 24	B-24L-1-CO	44-41395	**10**
A72-75: 7 OTU	B-24L-1-CO	44-41403	-
A72-76: 7 OTU, 25, 21, (24), 21	B-24L-1-CO	44-41402	**36**
A72-77: 7 OTU, 24	B-24L-1-CO	44-41404	**24#**
A72-78: 7 OTU, 24 *[GR-T]*, (21), 24	B-24L-1-CO	44-41405	**26**
A72-79: 7 OTU	B-24L-1-CO	44-41444	-
A72-80: 7 OTU, 24	B-24L-5-CO	44-41450	**16#**
A72-81: 7 OTU, 24 *[GR-T]*	B-24L-5-CO	44-41454	**17#**
A72-82: 7 OTU, 23, 82 Wing	B-24L-5-CO	44-41452	**20**
A72-83: -	B-24L-5-CO	44-41455	-
A72-84: 7 OTU, 24 *[GR-D]*, 23, 21, 82 Wing	B-24L-5-CO	44-41456	**33**
A72-85: 7 OTU, 1 ADTF	B-24L-5-CO	44-41457	-

A72-75 was a B-24L that served with 7 OTU between October 1944 and November 1945. *(AHM & WA)*

A72-86: 7 OTU, 23	B-24L-5-CO	44-41458	20
A72-87: 1 APU	B-24L-5-CO	44-41459	-
A72-88: 7 OTU, 24	B-24L-5-CO	44-41460	17
A72-89: 7 OTU, 25, 24, (*21*), 24	B-24L-10-CO	44-41575	24
A72-90: 7 OTU, 24, 23, 21	B-24L-10-CO	44-41579	10
A72-91: 7 OTU, 23, 21	B-24L-10-CO	44-41580	13
A72-92: 7 OTU, 25, 24, 21 *[MJ-D]*	B-24L-10-CO	44-41581	25#
A72-93: 7 OTU, 24	B-24L-10-CO	44-41582	21
A72-94: 7 OTU, 23, 21, (*24*), 21	B-24L-10-CO	44-41583	35
A72-95: 7 OTU, 24, (*21*), 24	B-24L-10-CO	44-41604	26
A72-96: 23	B-24L-15-CO	44-41653	14
A72-97: 7 OTU, 24, 23	B-24L-10-CO	44-41608	13
A72-98: 7 OTU, 23, 21	B-24L-10-CO	44-41639	20
A72-99: 7 OTU, 23, 24	B-24L-10-CO	44-41640	14
A72-100: 23, 24	B-24L-10-CO	44-41609	10
A72-101: 21 *[MJ-J]*	B-24L-15-CO	44-41654	2
A72-102: 23 *[NV-S]*, 24	B-24L-10-CO	44-41611	18
A72-103: 23, 24	B-24L-10-CO	44-41577	13
A72-104: 23	B-24L-10-CO	44-41612	12
A72-105: 7 OTU, 24, (*21*), 24, 23	B-24L-10-CO	44-41617	23
A72-106: 7 OTU, 24, (*23*), 24	B-24L-10-CO	44-41605	26
A72-107: 23, 24	B-24L-10-CO	44-41607	10
A72-108: 21	B-24L-10-CO	44-41618	16
A72-109: 7 OTU	B-24L-10-CO	44-41630	-
A72-110: 7 OTU	B-24L-15-CO	44-41656	-
A72-111: 7 OTU	B-24L-15-CO	44-41663	-
A72-112: 7 OTU	B-24L-15-CO	44-41664	-
A72-113: 7 OTU	B-24L-10-CO	44-41629	-
A72-114: 7 OTU	B-24L-10-CO	44-41633	-
A72-115: -	B-24L-10-CO	44-41632	-
A72-116: 7 OTU	B-24L-10-CO	44-41631	-
A72-117: 7 OTU	B-24L-10-CO	44-41634	-
A72-118: 7 OTU	B-24L-10-CO	44-41635	-
A72-119: 7 OTU	B-24L-10-CO	44-41636	-
A72-120: 7 OTU	B-24L-10-CO	44-41642	-
A72-121: 7 OTU	B-24L-15-CO	44-41666	-
A72-122: 7 OTU	B-24L-10-CO	44-41637	-
A72-123: 7 OTU	B-24L-10-CO	44-41638	-
A72-124: 25	B-24L-15-CO	44-41657	1#
A72-125: 7 OTU	B-24L-5-CO	44-41505	-
A72-126: 7 OTU	B-24L-5-CO	44-41499	-
A72-127: 7 OTU	B-24L-5-CO	44-41502	-
A72-128: 7 OTU	B-24L-5-CO	44-41503	-
A72-129: 7 OTU	B-24L-5-CO	44-41504	-
A72-130: 7 OTU	B-24L-5-CO	44-41506	-
A72-131: 7 OTU	B-24L-5-CO	44-41508	-
A72-132: 7 OTU	B-24L-5-CO	44-41507	-
A72-133: 7 OTU, 25	B-24L-5-CO	44-41509	3#
A72-134: 25	B-24L-5-CO	44-41510	2
A72-135: 7 OTU	B-24L-5-CO	44-41511	-
A72-136: 7 OTU	B-24L-5-CO	44-41512	-
A72-137: 25 *[SJ-K]*	B-24L-5-CO	44-41513	8
A72-138: 7 OTU	B-24L-5-CO	44-41514	-
A72-139: 7 OTU	B-24L-15-CO	44-41658	-
A72-140: 25 *[SJ-J]*	B-24L-15-CO	44-41665	9
A72-141: 99, 21	B-24L-15-CO	44-41677	3
A72-142: 7 OTU	B-24L-15-CO	44-41682	-
A72-143: 23, 12, 24, 21	B-24M-1-CO	44-41828	9
A72-144: 25 *[SJ-A]*	B-24M-1-CO	44-41831	8
A72-145: 12, 21, (*24*), 21	B24-M-1-CO	44-41834	16

A72-146: 7 OTU	B-24M-1-CO	44-41836	-
A72-147: 25 *[SJ-H]*	B-24M-5-CO	44-41885	**9**
A72-148: 12, 24, 21	B-24M-5-CO	44-41886	**31**
A72-149: 25 *[SJ-N]*	B-24L-5-CO	44-41515	**12**
A72-150: 25 *[SJ-L]*	B-24L-5-CO	44-41516	**4**
A72-151: 25 *[SJ-M]*	B-24L-5-CO	44-41517	**9**
A72-152: 25 *[SJ-F]*	B-24L-5-CO	44-41518	**6**
A72-153: 99, 21	B-24L-5-CO	44-41530	**14**
A72-154: 25 *[SJ-E]*	B-24L-5-CO	44-51531	**9**
A72-155: 23, 7 OTU	B-24L-5-CO	44-41532	-

B-24L A72-154 of 25 Sqn being serviced at Cunderdin in 1945. *(AHM & WA)*

A72-156: 25 *[SJ-D]*	B-24L-5-CO	44-41533	**3**
A72-157: 7 OTU	B-24L-5-CO	44-41529	-
A72-158: 12, 24	B-24M-10-CO	44-41971	**25**
A72-159: 200 Flt	B-24M-10-CO	44-41972	**1#**
A72-160: 12	B-24M-10-CO	44-41949	**1**
A72-161: 12, 24, 23, 21	B-24M-10-CO	44-41950	**12**
A72-162: 7 OTU	B-24M-10-CO	44-41951	-
A72-163: 12, 24	B-24M-10-CO	44-41952	**24**
A72-164: 7 OTU	B-24M-10-CO	44-41953	-
A72-165: 7 OTU, 25 *[SJ-Z]*	B-24M-10-CO	44-41954	**5**
A72-166: 12, 24 *[GR-X]*	B-24M-10-CO	44-41955	**18**
A72-167: 12, *(21)*, 12, 23, 24	B-24M-10-CO	44-41957	**21**
A72-168: 99, 24, *(23)*, *(21)*, 24	B-24M-10-CO	44-41958	**14**
A72-169: 200 Flt	B-24M-10-CO	44-41959	-
A72-170: 24, 23, 24	B-24M-10-CO	44-41960	**4**
A72-171: 12, 23, 24, 21	B-24M-10-CO	44-41961	**5**
A72-172: 1 CU	B-24M-10-CO	44-41962	-
A72-173: 12, 21, *(23)*, 21, 24	B-24M-10-CO	44-41963	**7**
A72-174: 200 Flt	B-24M-10-CO	44-41964	-
A72-175: 24, 23	B-24M-10-CO	44-41965	-
A72-176: 7 OTU	B-24M-10-CO	44-41966	-
A72-177: 200 Flt	B-24M-10-CO	44-41967	**1#**
A72-178: 99, 25	B-24M-10-CO	44-41968	-
A72-179: 24, 21	B-24M-10-CO	44-41969	**18**
A72-180: 200 Flt	B-24M-10-CO	44-41970	**12**
A72-181: 21	B-24M-10-CO	44-41973	-

A72-182: 200 Flt	B-24M-10-CO	44-41974	14
A72-183: 200 Flt *[NX-R]*	B-24M-10-CO	44-41975	14
A72-184: 24, *(21)*, 24	B-24M-10-CO	44-41976	5
A72-185: 7 OTU, 200 Flt	B-24M-10-CO	44-41977	2
A72-186: 201 Flt *[LV-A]*	B-24M-10-CO	44-41978	-
A72-187: 99, 200 Flt	B-24M-10-CO	44-41979	13
A72-188: 12, 23, 21	B-24M-10-CO	44-41980	7
A72-189: 11 CU, 82 Wing	B-24M-10-CO	44-41982	-
A72-190: 99, 25 *[SJ-Y]*	B-24M-10-CO	44-41983	4
A72-191: 200 Flt	B-24M-10-CO	44-41984	1#

B-24M A72-190 of 25 Sqn. It was allotted to this unit in May 1945. *(AHM & WA)*

A72-192: 200 Flt	B-24M-10-CO	44-41987	16
A72-193: 7 OTU, 1 CU, 21, 82 Wing	B-24M-10-CO	44-41988	-
A72-194: 99 *[UX-R]*, 24	B-24M-10-CO	44-41989	5
A72-195: 99, 200 Flt	B-24M-10-CO	44-41990	3
A72-196: 99, 24, *(21)*, 24	B-24M-10-CO	44-41991	14#
A72-197: 201 Flt *[LV-B]*	B-24M-10-CO	44-41992	-
A72-198: 1 APU	B-24M-10-CO	44-41993	-
A72-199 to A72-299 not allocated			
A72-300: 99, 23	B-24J-5-NT	44-28063	-
A72-301: 99	B-24J-5-NT	44-28064	-
A72-302: 99	B-24J-5-NT	44-28065	-
A72-303: 99, 21	B-24J-5-NT	44-28066	-
A72-304: 99	B-24J-5-NT	44-28067	-
A72-305: 99	B-24J-5-NT	44-28069	-
A72-306: 99	B-24J-5-NT	44-28087	-

A72-307: 99 *[UX-K]*, 21	B-24J-5-NT	44-28097	-
A72-308: 99	B-24J-5-NT	44-28099	-
A72-309: 99, 21	B-24J-5-NT	44-28101	-
A72-310: 12	B-24J-5-NT	44-28104	**13**
A72-311: 99 *[UX-O]*	B-24J-5-NT	44-28139	-
A72-312: 23, 24 *[GR-L]*	B-24J-5-NT	44-28086	-
A72-313: 99	B-24J-5-NT	44-28125	-
A72-314: 12	B-24J-5-NT	44-28127	**14#**
A72-315: 1 APU	B-24J-5-NT	44-28256	-
A72-316: 12	B-24J-5-NT	44-28079	**12**
A72-317: 12	B-24J-5-NT	44-28122	**4**
A72-318: 12, 99	B-24J-5-NT	44-28070	**11**
A72-319: 12	B-24J-5-NT	44-28082	**9**
A72-320: 12	B-24J-5-NT	44-28132	**10**
A72-321: 12	B-24J-5-NT	44-28089	7
A72-322: 12	B-24J-5-NT	44-28079	**11**
A72-323: 12	B-24J-5-NT	44-28103	7
A72-324: 12	B-24J-5-NT	44-28134	**1**
A72-325: 12	B-24J-5-NT	44-28107	**6**
A72-326: 12	B-24J-5-NT	44-28188	-
A72-327: 12	B-24J-5-NT	44-28123	-
A72-328: 12	B-24J-5-NT	44-28092	7
A72-329: 12	B-24J-5-NT	44-28100	7
A72-330: 12	B-24J-5-NT	44-28114	-
A72-331: 12	B-24J-5-NT	44-28068	-
A72-332: 99 *[UX-A]*, 23	B-24J-5-NT	44-28131	-
A72-333: 99, 21	B-24J-5-NT	44-28098	-
A72-334: 102	B-24J-5-NT	44-28091	-
A72-335: 102 *[BV-A]*	B-24J-5-NT	44-28081	-
A72-336: 102	B-24J-5-NT	44-28108	-
A72-337: 102	B-24J-5-NT	44-28078	-
A72-338: 102	B-24J-5-NT	44-10295	-
A72-339: 102	B-24J-5-NT	44-28124	-
A72-340: 102 *[BV-G]*	B-24J-5-NT	44-28096	-
A72-341: 102	B-24J-5-NT	44-28113	-
A72-342: 102	B-24J-5-NT	44-28137	-
A72-343: 102	B-24J-5-NT	44-28080	-
A72-344: 102	B-24J-5-NT	44-28106	-
A72-345: 102	B-24J-5-NT	44-28084	-
A72-346: 12	B-24J-5-NT	44-28126	-
A72-347: 12	B-24J-5-NT	44-28109	-
A72-348: 23	B-24J-5-NT	44-28072	-
A72-349: 23	B-24J-5-NT	44-28077	-
A72-350: 201 Flt	B-24J-5-NT	44-28090	-
A72-351: 23	B-24J-5-NT	44-28074	-
A72-352: 25	B-24J-5-NT	44-28135	-
A72-353: 25, 82 Wing	B-24J-5-NT	44-28133	-
A72-354: 23	B-24J-5-NT	44-28083	-
A72-355: 12	B-24J-5-NT	44-28085	-
A72-356: 23, 24	B-24J-5-NT	44-28130	-
A72-357: 201 Flt *[LV-D]*, 12	B-24J-5-NT	44-28129	-
A72-358: 99, 21	B-24J-5-NT	44-28093	-
A72-359: 23	B-24J-5-NT	44-28111	-
A72-360: 23	B-24J-5-NT	44-28128	-
A72-361: 12	B-24J-5-NT	44-28134	-
A72-362: 23, 82 Wing, 23 *[NV-K]*	B-24J-5-NT	44-28073	-
A72-363: 12	B-24J-5-NT	44-28149	-
A72-364: 99 *[UX-J]*	B-24J-5-NT	44-28168	-
A72-365: 12	B-24J-5-NT	44-28156	-
A72-366: 23	B-24J-1-NT	42-78787	-

Serial	Type	USAAF serial	
A72-367: 23	B-24J-5-NT	44-28088	-
A72-368: 23	B-24J-5-NT	44-28094	-
A72-369: 21	B-24J-5-NT	44-28136	-
A72-370: 82 Wing	B-24J-5-NT	44-28144	-
A72-371: -	B-24J-5-NT	44-28164	-
A72-372: 23	B-24J-5-NT	44-28140	-
A72-373: 200 Flt	B-24J-5-NT	44-28148	-
A72-374: 12	B-24J-5-NT	44-28071	-
A72-375: 82 Wing	B-24J-5-NT	44-28102	-
A72-376: -	B-24J-5-NT	44-28121	-
A72-377: -	B-24J-5-NT	44-28174	-
A72-378: -	B-24J-5-NT	44-28171	-
A72-379: 7 OTU	B-24J-5-NT	44-28143	-
A72-380: 7 OTU	B-24J-5-NT	44-28145	-
A72-381: CFS	B-24J-5-NT	44-28151	-
A72-382: -	B-24J-5-NT	44-28183	-
A72-383: CFS	B-24J-5-NT	44-28142	-
A72-384: 23, 82 Wing	B-24J-5-NT	44-28162	-
A72-385: 82 Wing	B-24J-5-NT	44-28179	-
A72-386: HQ Sqn East Sale	B-24J-5-NT	44-28155	-
A72-387: 7 OTU	B-24J-5-NT	44-28062	-
A72-388: 23	B-24J-5-NT	44-28169	-
A72-389: 21	B-24J-5-NT	44-28167	-
A72-390: -	B-24J-5-NT	44-28166	-
A72-391: -	B-24J-5-NT	44-28146	-
A72-392: -	B-24J-5-NT	44-28178	-
A72-393: -	B-24J-5-NT	44-28075	-
A72-394: -	B-24J-5-NT	44-28159	-
A72-395: -	B-24J-5-NT	44-28180	-
A72-396: -	B-24J-5-NT	44-28172	-
A72-397: -	B-24J-5-NT	44-28175	-
A72-398: -	B-24J-5-NT	44-28158	-
A72-399: -	B-24J-5-NT	44-28150	-
A72-400: -	B-24J-5-NT	44-28147	-
A72-401: 12 *[NH-L]*	B-24J-5-NT	44-28153	-
A72-402: -	B-24J-5-NT	44-28160	-
A72-403: -	B-24J-5-NT	44-28161	-
A72-404: -	B-24J-1-NT	42-78726	-
A72-405: -	B-24J-1-NT	42-78727	-

Two more B-24J-5-NTs allocated to the RAAF were never taken on charge, 44-28105, lost between Long Beach (CA) and Hickam (HI) on 20 May 1945 and 44-28157 written-off after an engine fire on ground on 21 August 1945 prior to delivery to Australia.

Uncounted sorties: 'NV-R' - 23 Sqn (1), '986' - 24 Sqn (1) and 14 for 21 Sqn.

✝

IN MEMORIAM

Consolidated B-24 Liberator (as an aircrew)
RAAF

Name	Service No	Rank	Age	Origin	Date	Serial
ALLEN, Thomas Walter	Aus. 440166	F/Sgt	19	RAAF	20.05.45	A72-160
ANDERSON, John Colin William	Aus. 424011	F/Sgt	26	RAAF	21.05.45	A72-177
ANDREWS, Athol Martin	Aus. 412351	F/L	21	RAAF	02.07.45	A72-64
ANSTEY, Frederick William*	Aus. 116993	Sgt	21	RAAF	29.10.44	42-110120
BADGER, Neil Thomas**	Aus. 407161	F/L	27	RAAF	08.05.44	42-41117
BAILE, Evelyn Bruce	Aus. 415603	W/O	24	RAAF	23.01.45	A72-70
BAILEY, Lester Maxwell	Aus. 443477	F/Sgt	31	RAAF	20.05.45	A72-160
BANKS, Ronald Joseph	Aus. 436999	F/Sgt	23	RAAF	06.04.45	A72-81
BARBER, William Ronald*	Aus. 423587	F/Sgt	20	RAAF	29.10.44	42-110120
BARDWELL, Harley Russell	Aus. 419950	W/O	31	RAAF	01.07.45	A72-61
BEATTIE, Roy Mcdowall	Aus. 404228	F/L	24	RAAF	02.07.45	A72-64
BELL, William Samuel	Aus. 417693	F/O	25	RAAF	20.05.45	A72-160
BENSON, Donald Douglas	Aus. 435604	F/Sgt	19	RAAF	20.05.45	A72-160
BEVAN, Keith Harry**	Aus. 35952	P/O	22	RAAF	23.11.43	42-40967
BILTOFT, Tom Tate	Aus. 404525	F/O	28	RAAF	17.05.45	A72-159
BIRD, Walter James*	Aus. 62526	Sgt	22	RAAF	29.10.44	42-110120
BOWEN, Trevor Edward	Aus. 439863	F/Sgt	19	RAAF	06.04.45	A72-81
BOYD, Harry James	Aus. 427775	F/Sgt	22	RAAF	23.03.45	A72-80
BROWN, Kelvin Arthur Roy	Aus. 426804	F/O	27	RAAF	06.04.45	A72-81
BROWN, Lionel James	Aus. 413536	F/O	26	RAAF	17.05.45	A72-159
BURGESS, Aubrey Edward	Aus. 443659	F/Sgt	32	RAAF	31.07.45	A72-66
BURROWS, Martin Allan	Aus. 12720	P/O	28	RAAF	05.07.45	A72-196
CAMPBELL, Henry Rupert	Aus. 411860	F/L	22	RAAF	17.05.45	A72-159
CARLSON, Eric Ferdinand	Aus. 424965	W/O	27	RAAF	18.08.45	A72-306
CLARK, Archibald Mclaren	Aus. 402309	F/O	24	RAAF	17.05.45	A72-159
CLARK, Herbert James	Aus. 413153	F/O	24	RAAF	17.05.45	A72-159
CLAUSEN, Arthur Kevin	Aus. 439868	F/Sgt	22	RAAF	16.08.45	A72-306
CLOAKE, Stephen Patrick	Aus. 441014	F/Sgt	20	RAAF	27.07.45	A72-92
COLLINS, Alan Noel John	Aus. 424373	W/O	21	RAAF	06.04.45	A72-77
COOK, Alfred	Aus. 419295	W/O	30	RAAF	27.07.45	A72-92
COOK, James Edward*	Aus. 429432	F/Sgt	24	RAAF	29.10.44	42-110120
CORMACK, Philip Hector	Aus. 421295	W/O	23	RAAF	21.05.45	A72-177
CORNELIUS, Ronald Michael	Aus. 436789	F/Sgt	20	RAAF	05.07.45	A72-196
CORNES, William James	Aus. 435651	F/Sgt	23	RAAF	23.01.45	A72-70
COX, Bernard Leslie	Aus. 412402	W/O	26	RAAF	20.05.45	A72-160
COX, Charles Ian	Aus. 415403	F/O	22	RAAF	25.03.45	A72-191
CROPLEY, Alan Arthur*	Aus. 416078	F/L	23	RAAF	29.10.44	42-110120
CROWTHER, Lance Dixon	Aus. 403560	F/L	26	RAAF	06.04.45	A72-77
DAVERN, Owen William John	Aus. 5312	F/Sgt	32	RAAF	21.05.45	A72-177
DAVIDSON, Stuart Hugh*	Aus. 413969	W/O	23	RAAF	29.10.44	42-110120
DAVIS, Allan	Aus. 431280	F/Sgt	19	RAAF	06.04.45	A72-81
DAY, Leonard Francis	Aus. 409672	F/L	26	RAAF	25.03.45	A72-191
DELAHUNT, Robert William	Aus. 439573	F/Sgt	20	RAAF	31.07.45	A72-66
DEVEREUX, Leslie William	Aus. 438586	F/Sgt	20	RAAF	02.07.45	A72-64

Name	Service No.	Rank	Age	Service	Date	Aircraft
DEWHURST, Douglas Poultney	AUS. 403780	F/O	25	RAAF	31.07.45	A72-66
DUCANSON, Leonard	AUS. 59752	Sgt	24	RAAF	20.05.45	A72-160
DUREAU, George Alfred	AUS. 13926	Sgt	30	RAAF	14.09.45	A72-313
EASTON, Ivan Nelson Luke	AUS. 439751	F/Sgt	19	RAAF	20.05.45	A72-160
EDWARDS, Kenneth William	AUS. 400053	F/L	30	RAAF	23.01.45	A72-70
EMMETT, Keith Roy Norman	AUS. 411761	F/L	25	RAAF	21.05.45	A72-177
EVANS, Thomas Guy	AUS. 401186	F/L	23	RAAF	23.01.45	A72-70
FAICHNIE, Ian	AUS. 431408	F/L	19	RAAF	06.04.45	A72-77
FAVIELL, Jack Bonfield	AUS. 403916	F/O	29	RAAF	31.07.45	A72-66
FEATHERSTONE, Dennis Geoffrey	AUS. 438726	F/Sgt	19	RAAF	02.07.45	A72-64
FLANAGAN, William Richard	AUS. 401748	W/O	26	RAAF	23.03.45	A72-80
FORD, Eric Valentine	AUS. 255138	F/L	34	RAAF	06.04.45	A72-77
GAMBLE, Clarence Augustine Reginald	AUS. 439646	F/Sgt	19	RAAF	17.05.45	A72-159
GOODING, Harold Allan	AUS. 418040	W/O	25	RAAF	05.07.45	A72-196
GRADWELL, David Prenton	AUS. 8960	F/L	25	RAAF	25.03.45	A72-191
GRAHAM, John Oswald	AUS. 418101	F/L	28	RAAF	21.05.45	A72-177
HALE, Robert Roland	AUS. 444233	Sgt	19	RAAF	25.03.45	A72-191
HANSON, Kenneth John	AUS. 403585	F/L	27	RAAF	27.07.45	A72-92
HARRISON, Alan Lindsey*	AUS. 408190	F/O	29	RAAF	29.10.44	42-110120
HEAD, Graham Neil	AUS. 431625	F/Sgt	19	RAAF	23.01.45	A72-70
HENDY, George Allan	AUS. 401441	F/L	28	RAAF	14.09.45	A72-313
HERBERT, Donald Norrie	AUS. 433297	F/Sgt	21	RAAF	09.10.44	44-40398
HERPS, John Raymond Wilbur	AUS. 440858	F/Sgt	25	RAAF	20.05.45	A72-160
HESLIN, Bredan Michael	AUS. 440787	F/Sgt	21	RAAF	27.07.45	A72-92
HIGGINBOTTOM, Roy	AUS. 8503	Sgt	23	RAAF	14.02.45	A72-124
HOCKINGS, Thomas	AUS. 425936	F/O	34	RAAF	02.07.45	A72-64
HOGG, Arthur James	AUS. 430751	F/Sgt	20	RAAF	02.07.45	A72-64
HOLLIS, John Austin	AUS. 445226	F/Sgt	19	RAAF	20.05.45	A72-160
HOLOHAN, Joseph	AUS. 412532	Sgt	21	RAAF	11.06.43	42-40500
HOLT, Jack	AUS. 412142	W/O	22	RAAF	23.01.45	A72-70
HUME, John James Oliver	AUS. 427095	F/O	28	RAAF	27.07.45	A72-92
HURSTHOUSE, John Wilson	AUS. 416215	F/O	31	RAAF	23.03.45	A72-80
HUTTON, Frank Grainger Vincent	AUS. 437421	F/Sgt	23	RAAF	27.07.45	A72-92
JAMIESON, Stewart Hugh*	AUS. 36474	Sgt	24	RAAF	29.10.44	42-110120
JOHNSON, Brian John Troy	AUS. 444015	Sgt	19	RAAF	14.02.45	A72-124
JOHNSTON, Raymond Dalwood	AUS. 445230	Sgt	18	RAAF	15.02.45	A72-112
JONES, Allen Leslie	AUS. 14233	W/O	24	RAAF	14.02.45	A72-112
JONES, Herbert Archibald John	AUS. 411222	F/O	26	RAAF	17.05.45	A72-159
JORDAN, Bernard Thomas	AUS. 407825	F/O	29	RAAF	06.04.45	A72-77
KILLEN, Keith Leonard James*	AUS. 416861	W/O	23	RAAF	29.10.44	42-110120
KYLE-LITTLE, David Knox	AUS. 6584	Sgt	24	RAAF	23.01.45	A72-70
LAING, William	AUS. 406568	F/L	26	RAAF	06.04.45	A72-77
LINDLEY, George Grey	AUS. 427712	P/O	21	RAAF	27.07.45	A72-92
LITCHFIELD, Eric Mileham	AUS. 439370	Sgt	20	RAAF	25.03.45	A72-191
LOCKYER, Arnold Alexander	AUS. 80471	F/Sgt	30	RAAF	21.08.45	A72-92
LOW, Kevin Marvyn	AUS. 435733	Sgt	19	RAAF	25.03.45	A72-191
MADDEN, Douglas William	AUS. 36484	Cpl	22	RAAF	23.02.45	A72-80
MANNING, Colin Montague	AUS. 409282	F/O	29	RAAF	17.05.45	A72-159
MARTIN, Dennis Lodge	AUS. 8811	F/Sgt	29	RAAF	01.07.45	A72-61
MARTIN, Noel Patrick	AUS. 433734	F/Sgt	19	RAAF	23.01.45	A72-70
MATTHEWS, Philip William	AUS. 406080	F/L	29	RAAF	09.04.46	A72-348
MAXWELL, William James	AUS. 435994	F/Sgt	20	RAAF	27.07.45	A72-92
McDONALD, Sidney Leonard	AUS. 411524	F/L	28	RAAF	06.04.45	A72-81
McLEAN, Donald	AUS. 78	G/C	31	RAAF	01.07.45	A72-61
MIDDLETON, Bertram John***	AUS. 408052	P/O	25	RAAF	05.08.44	A72-41
MORRIS, Ronald Malcolm	AUS. 46563	F/Sgt	21	RAAF	23.03.45	A72-80
MOUATT, Peter Albert	AUS. 405523	F/O	22	RAAF	06.04.45	A72-81
MUTTON, James Harold	AUS. 34046	F/O	32	RAAF	14.09.45	A72-313

Naughton, Francis Joseph	Aus. 449767	Sgt	22	RAAF	14.02.45	A72-124
Nichol, Charles Neville*	Aus. 440381	F/Sgt	20	RAAF	27.07.45	A72-92
O'Dea, Donald John	Aus. 408590	F/O	21	RAAF	29.10.42	42-110120
Orgill, John Victor	Aus. 441469	F/Sgt	22	RAAF	28.07.45	A72-92
Paech, Bruce Vaughton	Aus. 416188	W/O	29	RAAF	31.07.45	A72-66
Parker, Herbert Gordon	Aus. 408591	W/O	25	RAAF	23.03.45	A72-80
Parkinson, John Richard	Aus. 411371	F/L	27	RAAF	02.02.45	A72-88
Parry-Okeden, Charles David	Aus. 404485	F/L	22	RAAF	23.03.45	A72-80
Patten, Keith Lawrence	Aus. 440006	F/Sgt	20	RAAF	02.07.45	A72-64
Playford, Neville Herbert	Aus. 439635	F/Sgt	20	RAAF	31.07.45	A72-66
Pitt, John McPherson	Aus. 401830	F/O	26	RAAF	02.02.45	A72-88
Pockley, Harold Graham	Aus. 260608	S/L	32	RAAF	25.03.45	A72-191
Ponting, Charles Kevin	Aus. 434348	Sgt	21	RAAF	25.03.45	A72-191
Proudlock, Ralph	Aus. 420488	Sgt	22	RAAF	21.05.45	A72-177
Pullin, Raymond Frank	Aus. 411050	F/O	29	RAAF	14.09.45	A72-313
Quinn, Vincent John	Aus. 437876	F/Sgt	23	RAAF	14.09.45	A72-313
Raine, Leslie	Aus. 439612	F/Sgt	19	RAAF	06.04.45	A72-77
Redman, John Robert Walter	Aus. 402395	S/L	30	RAAF	05.07.45	A72-196
Rice, John William	Aus. 412186	F/L	28	RAAF	17.05.45	A72-159
Richards, Kenwyn Howard	Aus. 407253	P/O	29	RAAF	23.01.45	A72-70
Riley, Harry	Aus. 14457	Sgt	30	RAAF	17.05.45	A72-159
Robinson, Ronald Walpole Buist	Aus. 14526	Cpl	28	RAAF	02.07.45	A72-64
Rodgers, William Anthony Jordan	Aus. 436889	F/Sgt	22	RAAF	23.03.45	A72-80
Rogers, Leslie	Aus. 449787	F/Sgt	26	RAAF	05.07.45	A72-196
Rollings, Frederick Leslie	Aus. 438085	F/Sgt	24	RAAF	05.07.45	A72-196
Roy, John Alfred	Aus. 266200	F/L	40	RAAF	01.07.45	A72-61
Rust, Thomas Nathan	Aus. 408378	W/O	32	RAAF	20.05.45	A72-160
Ryan, John Richmond	Aus. 422716	F/Sgt	22	RAAF	23.03.45	A72-80
Sapwell, Leonrad Robert	Aus. 116599	F/Sgt	20	RAAF	02.07.45	A72-64
Scott, Gordon Malcolm	Aus. 23277	Sgt	26	RAAF	31.07.45	A72-66
Shadforth, Harold	Aus. 449303	F/Sgt	29	RAAF	05.07.45	A72-196
Shorter, Ernest Travers	Aus. 14791	W/O	27	RAAF	21.05.45	A72-177
Sismey, Francis Leonard	Aus. 402764	F/L	26	RAAF	20.05.45	A72-160
Skinner, Rex Victor	Aus. 407185	F/L	26	RAAF	05.07.45	A72-196
Stanley, Patrick Fraser	Aus. 430846	F/Sgt	23	RAAF	05.07.45	A72-196
Starr, Lawrence James	Aus. 71522	Sgt	22	RAAF	21.05.45	A72-177
Stroud, Harry	Aus. 403768	F/L	30	RAAF	02.07.45	A72-64
Stevenson, Joseph Arthur William	Aus. 425068	F/Sgt	30	RAAF	23.01.45	A72-70
Straus, Nathaniel Ivan	Aus. 250759	S/L	32	RAAF	23.03.45	A72-80
Stubbs, William Joseph	Aus. 418199	F/O	22	RAAF	31.07.45	A72-66
Tapper, Roy	Aus. 434336	F/Sgt	28	RAAF	05.07.45	A72-196
Taylor, Charles Ronald	Aus. 41804	Sgt	22	RAAF	14.02.45	A72-124
Taylor, Reginald Lee	Aus. 120044	F/O	31	RAAF	21.05.45	A72-177
Teitzel, Leonard King	Aus. 405430	P/O	27	RAAF	23.01.45	A72-70
Theyer, Ernest Frederick	Aus. 422755	F/L	26	RAAF	21.05.45	A72-177
Thomson, John Stanley	Aus. 438719	F/Sgt	21	RAAF	06.04.45	A72-81
Tonkin, Leslie Ernest	Aus. 443698	Sgt	19	RAAF	25.03.45	A72-191
Uhr, Kenneth William	Aus. 433831	F/Sgt	19	RAAF	14.02.45	A72-124
Vickers, James Olgive Ross	Aus. 66185	F/Sgt	21	RAAF	05.07.45	A72-196
Waddell, John Munro	Aus. 443444	F/Sgt	19	RAAF	06.04.45	A72-77
Walker, Rodney Nelson	Aus. 421421	F/L	24	RAAF	21.05.45	A72-177
Walker, Ronald Jack	Aus. 439333	F/Sgt	30	RAAF	31.07.45	A72-66
Walmsley, Leslie Kenneth	Aus. 435740	F/Sgt	19	RAAF	06.04.45	A72-81
Whitehead, Alexander Douglas	Aus. 121596	Sgt	20	RAAF	23.03.45	A72-80
White, Keith Jowett	Aus. 433632	F/Sgt	21	RAAF	06.04.45	A72-77
Whiting, Raymon Allenby	Aus. 426733	F/O	23	RAAF	23.03.45	A72-80
Wignall, Walter Joseph	Aus. 17299	Sgt	18	RAAF	06.04.45	A72-81
Wilken, Charles Leslie*	Aus. 408448	F/Sgt	22	RAAF	29.10.44	42-110120

WILLETT, Douglas William	AUS. 404424	F/L	29	RAAF	02.07.45	A72-64
WILMHURST, Kenneth Charles	AUS. 28787	Sgt	30	RAAF	25.03.45	A72-191
WORLEY, Alexander George	AUS. 435236	F/O	25	RAAF	06.04.45	A72-81

Total: 162

**530th BS/380th BG, **528th BS/380th BG*
****Killed in action but the aircraft was repaired and returned to service*

n/k: not known

Wreckage of A72-306/UX-J in which two crewmembers lost their lives, W/O E.F. Carlson and F/Sgt A.K. Clausen. Also, two of the eleven passengers were killed, Corporals J.R. Row and E.T. Sharpe both of the Women's Auxiliary Australian Air Force.

Wreckage of A72-112 of 7 OTU. Two crewmembers found death in the crash.

**Consolidated B-24D-20-CO Liberator A72-10
(ex-41-24127)**
No. 7 OTU RAAF
Tocumwal (NSW - Australia), spring 1944

**Consolidated B-24M-10-CO Liberator A72-179
(ex-44-41969)**
No. 21 Squadron RAAF
Balikpapan (Borneo), September 1945

**Consolidated B-24J-200-CO Liberator A72-54
(ex-44-41196)**

No. 24 Squadron RAAF
Fenton (NT - Australia), spring 1945

Consolidated B-24L-5-CO Liberator A72-84
(ex-44-41456)
No. 24 Squadron RAAF
Fenton (NT - Australia), spring 1945

**Consolidated B-24L-5-CO Liberator A72-150
(ex-44-41516)**
No. 25 Squadron RAAF
Cunderlin (WA - Australia), early 1945

Tail marking of No. 21 Squadron RAAF

Tail marking of No. 23 Squadron RAAF

Tail marking of No. 24 Squadron RAAF

Tail marking of No. 25 Squadron RAAF

Tail marking of No. 99 Squadron RAAF

Tail marking of No. 102 Squadron RAAF

SQUADRONS! - The series

SQUADRONS!
No.54
Phil H. LISTEMANN
The Hawker
Biplane Fighters

AT WAR:
STUDY, HISTORY AND STATISTICS
No.137 Squadron
1941 - 1945
COMPILED BY
H. LISTEMANN
WITH
CHRIS THOMAS

USN AIRCRAFT
1922-1962
Vol.7:
Designation Letter
'F' (Pt-4)

James Edgar JOHNSON DSO** DFC*
Supermarine Spitfire Mk.XIV MV257
No. 125 Wing
Group Captain J. E. Johnson
RAF No. 85267
B.160/Kastrup (Denmark), June 1945

www.RAF-IN-COMBAT.com
- USN Aircraft 1922-1962 -
- Squadrons! -
- RAF, Dominion and Allied squadrons at War -
- Allied Wings -
- Fighter Leaders -
- Prints (Aces and Leaders) -

Fighter Leaders
of the RAF, RAAF, RCAF, RNZAF & RAAF in WWII
Volume VII
Phil H. Listemann

ALLIED WINGS
No.19
Electric CANBERRA

SQUADRON
No.17
Phil H. LIST
The Curtiss
Mohawk